Tales We Heard on the Silk Road

Tales We Heard on the Silk Road

Plays, Puppet Shows, and Readers' Theater for Children

Stories from Attar, Rumi, and Saadi

Adapted for the stage by Nabeela M. Rehman

© 2015 by Nabeela M. Rehman. Willowbrook, Illinois, USA.

All rights reserved. This publication is protected by Copyright and written permission should be obtained from the author prior to any prohibited reproduction, storage or transmission.

Library of Congress Control Number: 2015919866
CreateSpace Independent Publishing Platform, North Charleston, SC

Author contact email: nabeelar@hotmail.com

Rehman, Nabeela M.
        Tales We Heard on the Silk Road: Plays, Puppet Shows, and Reader's Theater for Children / by Nabeela M. Rehman

ISBN-13: 978-1519461650
ISBN-10:1519461658

For Abid, Habib, and Zaynab

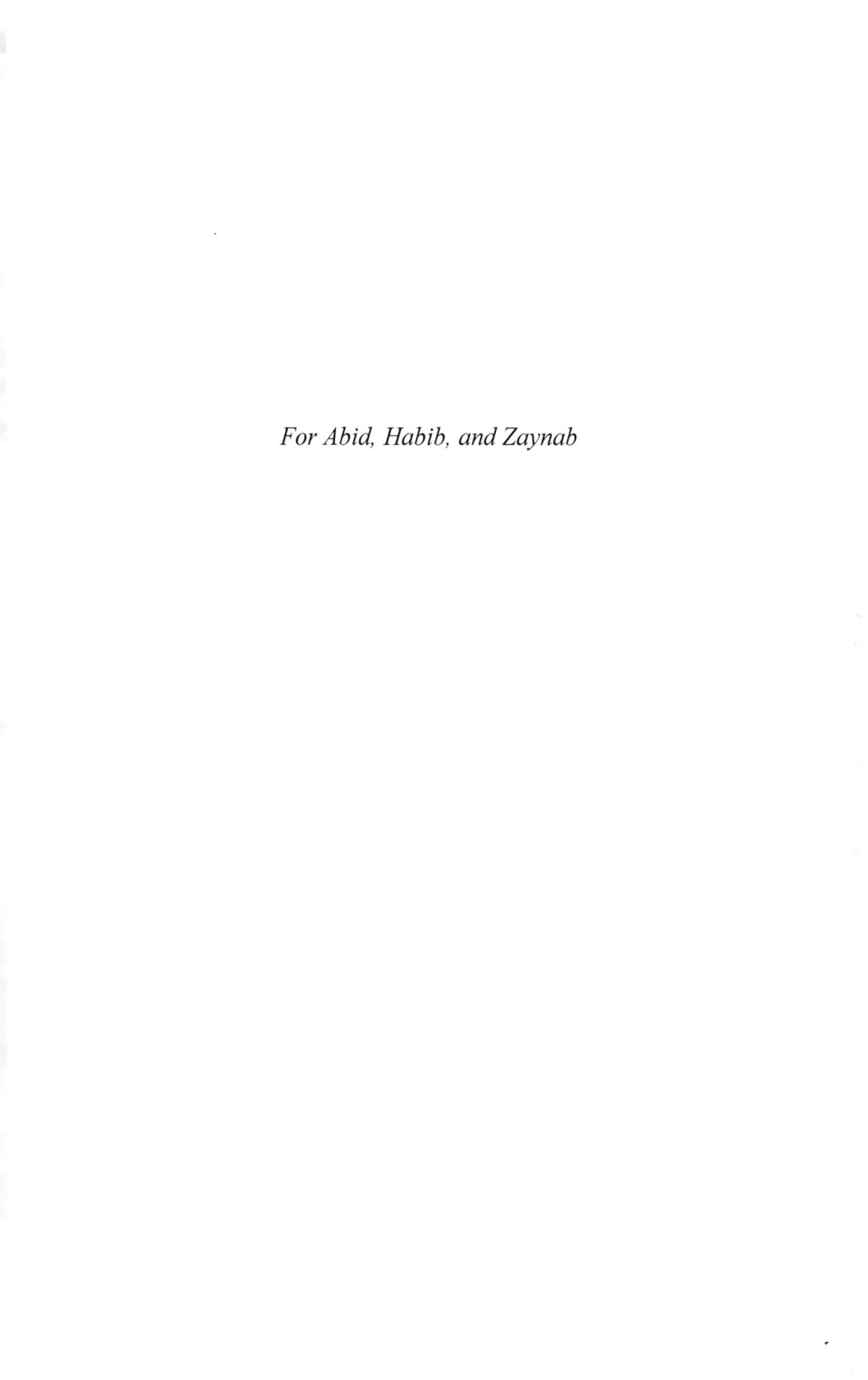

Table of Contents

Introduction... 3

Plays

The Elephant in the Dark (Rumi) 6

The Language of Animals (Rumi)............…........……… 17

Destiny at Sea (Saadi)……..................................... 41

The Middle Way (Attar)…....................................... 50

A Beggar's Remedy (Attar)….................................. 61

The Packsaddle Maker's School (Saadi).................... 89

Puppet Shows

A Lion Without a Mane or a Tail (Rumi).................. 112

The Unfair Verdict (Rumi)….................................. 117

Readers' Theater

The Old Woman's Cat 124

The Ailing Eyes….. 130

The Duck's Mistake…... 133

The Nightingale's Quick Wit…................…............. 136

The Sin of the Hen………………………..…………….. 140

The World-Traveling Pigeon……………………………. 144

Cooperation ……………………………………….…… 153

Introduction

Farid ad-Din Attar (1145-1221 CE) was born in Kadkhan near Nishapur in Iran. He was a perfume maker, pharmacist, and poet. Attar traveled to Baghdad, Mecca, Rey, Damascus, Egypt, Turkestan, and India. One of his many teachers was Shaykh Majd al Din Baghdadi. Attar is most well-known for his work *The Conference of the Birds (Manteq at-Tair)* as well as his hagiographic work *Memorials of the Saints (Tadghkirat al-Auliya)*. Attar's poems were translated into Persian prose by Mehdi Azar-Yazdi. English translations of these prose stories can be found in Muhammad Nur Abdus Salam's *Attar Stories for Young Adults* (ABC International Group, 2000).

Jalal ad-Din Rumi (1207-1273 CE) was born in Balkh in present-day Afghanistan, but his family settled in Konya, Turkey, due to Mongol invasions and unrest. He was trained as a teacher and jurist, but a meeting with Shams al-din of Tabriz ignited a friendship that would later inspire remarkable poetry. Rumi's greatest masterpiece is considered the *Mathnawi-yi-manawi*, a work consisting of more than 25,000 couplets. The plays in this collection have been drawn from Rumi's *Mathnawi*, as translated by Muhammad Nur Abdus Salam in *Rumi Stories for Young Adults from the Mathnawi* (ABC International Group, 2000).

Musharif-ud-Din Muslih-ud-Din Saadi (1210-1292 CE) was born in Shiraz, Iran. He established lyric poetry (*ghazals*) in Persian. His most famous works are *The Fruit Garden* (*Bustan*) and *The Rose Garden* (*Gulistan*). These are structured as collections of stories and anecdotes written in prose but interspersed with short sections of verse. Saadi traveled extensively, visiting Turkey, Syria, Iraq, Egypt, and North Africa, and is said to have traveled to Central Asia and India. He was even held prisoner by the Crusaders in Tripoli for a few years. "Fate" is from the *Gulistan* itself, and "The Packsaddle Maker's School" is based on a 19th century Persian revivalist interpretation of classical literature by Mehdi Azar-Yazdi. The English translation and prose adaptation of these stories is in Muhammad Nur Abdus Salam's *Saadi Stories for Young Adults from the Gulistan and other Works* (ABC International Group, 2001).

The puppet shows have been written so that no more than four characters are on stage at one time, i.e. two puppeteers with a puppet on each hand.

Readers' Theater is performed with children holding the scripts and reading from the scripts. There is no blocking/choreography required, making the performance easier for younger children. The Readers' Theater plays are derived from "Kalilah and Dimnah," stories translated and adapted from the Persian by Muhammad Nur Abdus Salam

"Kalilah and Dimnah" (ABC International Group, 2000) is a collection of fables. Kalilah and Dimnah are jackals who advise a lion king. They tell the lion king stories to teach him about political wisdom and cunning. Most of the characters are animals. The collection is believed to have been written in Sanskrit over 2,500 years ago in India. The stories were brought to Iran by the Sassanid king Anushirvan and translated into Pahlavi (Middle Persian). The stories have gone through a number of translations and revisions throughout history. The Persian translation and adaptation by Abu'l Maali Nasr Allah ibn Muhammad is considered a masterpiece of Persian literature. The first example of storytelling in Spanish, 1251 CE, was a translation of "Kalilah and Dimnah" from Ibn Muqaffa's Arabic version.

The Elephant in the Dark

Based on a short story by Rumi

Cast
The Villagers

TANGEH   Pronounced "Tang –ee," his name means "legs" in Urdu. In his 50s, pompous, formal, used to getting his own way; the richest and most influential person in the village.

SMALL BOY   A boy (or girl) about 6 to 8 years old.

PETEORPAYT   Pronounced "Pete-or-pay-t," his name means "back and belly" in Punjabi. In his 30s, easily excitable and emotional, somewhat wealthy, but he is propped up by his friends.

AHEER   His name means "end" in Urdu. In his 40s, stubborn, second richest man in town; he competes with Tangeh.

NAK   Her name means "nose" in Urdu. In her 50s, pokes her nose into everyone's business, suspicious, the village gossip.

KANN   Her name means "ear" in Urdu. In her 50s, overly sensitive widow, Nak's best friend.

DAND   Her name means "tooth" in Urdu.
                                  In her 40s, cares about her status,
                                  nouveau-riche mindset, wealthy.

LUQMAN   In his 20s, eager to learn, quiet, a
                                  bookworm, a bit timid but not shy
                                  when it comes to obtaining
                                  knowledge.

SOPHIA   In her 40s, self-assured, jovial,
                                  not really accepted by the
                                  villagers, but it doesn't bother her
                                  because as an outsider she feels
                                  she has more freedom. She loves
                                  freedom.

VILLAGE EXTRAS in last scene.

Elephant Handlers
BABAR   In his 50s, experienced animal
                                  trainer. He likes animals better
                                  than people.

JAMILLA   In her 30s, always paying
                                  attention to the money. She is
                                  rough, a survivor, the pragmatic
                                  business manager.

ALI   In his 20s, loud personality, the
                                  publicity man for the troupe.

Production Notes:

In the last part of the play, TANGEH, PETEORPAYT, AHEER, NAK, KANN, and DAND will put together a large elephant puppet. The piece of the puppet they hold should roughly correspond to their name (i.e., TANGEH holds the legs, DAND holds the tusk/head, etc.).

Scene 1. Setting: Outskirts of a village; SOPHIA's house and barn. The entrance to a barn is in one corner. A big empty yard is in the middle of the stage; the corner of a house is on the other side of the stage.

Near the house, TANGEH *and* SMALL BOY *are trying to hide.*

BABAR, JAMILLA, *and* ALI *exit the barn wearing colorful Punjabi clothing. They set down drums, flutes, flags, and large packs. They walk across the yard and go inside the house.*

TANGEH: So it's really true. They are here!

SMALL BOY: This is what I told you. Now you believe me. Omer saw them riding in! He told Nadia; I've told you.

TANGEH: Aside from Omer, no one else has actually seen the elephant?

SMALL BOY: As far as I know. You would be the first grown-up in the village to see it.

TANGEH: This is very good. I'll be able to tell everyone that I saw the elephant before anyone else! Now here is a copper piece; you run along home.

SMALL BOY *leaves.* NAK, KANN, DAND, PETEORPAYT, AHEER, *and* LUQMAN *arrive. They look at each other suspiciously, then pretend to ignore each other and act as if they are out for a nature walk. Finally,* TANGEH *knocks on the door. As soon as he does that, the rest of them gather around the door.*

SOPHIA: *(Behind door, not opening it.)* Who are you? What do you want? Why do you keep knocking at my door?

TANGEH: We want to see the elephant.

SOPHIA: Wait until tomorrow.

TANGEH: Sophia, let us in! We demand to see the Elephant Handlers. Otherwise I'll keep knocking on the door all night, and you won't get any sleep.

SOPHIA: *(Opening door.)* I might have known it was you Tangeh. And the rest of you lot — Peteorpayt, Aheer, Nak, Kann, Dand, and Luqman? Luqman, I'm surprised at you! Out making trouble tonight?

TANGEH: Now see here Sophia! We are respectable citizens, and we have important business to discuss with the Elephant Handlers. While we appreciate your hospitality in hosting them and their magnificent beast, we must speak to them on a matter of great importance.

SOPHIA: Great importance?

TANGEH: Great importance and extreme urgency, Sophia! *(The crowd nods and murmurs in agreement.)*

SOPHIA: Well, I have my doubts. But as you wish, respectable citizens. One moment. *(Closes door. After a few minutes door opens with* BABAR, JAMILLA, *and* ALI.*)*

TANGEH: Are you the Elephant Handlers?

BABAR: Yes. What is that to you?

TANGEH: We must see the elephant tonight.

JAMILLA: We're tired. We have traveled a long way. You'll all see the elephant tomorrow.

PETEORPAYT: We want to see the beast tonight!

ALI: The exhibition isn't ready. It would be better if you came back tomorrow.

AHEER: No! We won't leave until we see the elephant!

NAK: We are supporters of elephants and elephant arts and culture. We absolutely must see the elephant this very night.

BABAR: Please. It isn't possible. The elephant needs to sleep

DAND: We'll be very quiet so as not to wake him up.

BABAR: There's no light in the elephant's stable.

TANGEH: That doesn't matter. We can examine it even in the darkness.

KANN: We won't be able to sleep if we don't get to see the elephant tonight!

DAND: We have to see it before anyone else. We must be the first ones.

JAMILLA: Very well. If you are in such a hurry, the ticket on the opening night costs twice as much as on the other days.

AHEER: No problem. We'll pay three times as much.

BABAR: You'll have no more than one minute to look at it.

TANGEH: We agree! Even one minute is worth the trouble.

PETEORPAYT: If you want to beat us, we'll let you. We want the elephant. The elephant or death!

ALL VILLAGERS: Elephant or death! Elephant or death! Elephant or death!

BABAR: Calm down, calm down. Jamilla, collect their money. Ali, you guide them through the barn. Be careful, it is quite dark. Don't light a lamp; it will disturb Hahti Bhai.

All the villagers give their money to JAMILLA. *They all follow* ALI *into the barn, except* LUQMAN. JAMILLA *and* BABAR *are counting out money.* BABAR *looks up and notices* LUQMAN.

BABAR: Why don't you go in?

LUQMAN: I would like to visit the elephant before the others, but I can't see in the dark. So what's the point?

BABAR: (*Looks at JAMILLA.*) Exactly.

JAMILLA shrugs her shoulders noncommittally and continues to count coins.

LUQMAN: Please, you who know elephants better than anyone else, be my teacher for a moment and describe it.

JAMILLA: So you want to learn about elephants?

LUQMAN: Yes, please.

JAMILLA: Congratulations! It appears what we have here is a man of understanding!

LUQMAN: I have read a lot of books about elephants.

JAMILLA: The way to learn is like this: First you ask for information from people who know more than you do. Then you read books and learn what others have learned and understood. You research more, and in that way understand more.

BABAR: The elephant is an animal like a horse or a camel but much bigger and heavier. The difference between an elephant and a horse or camel is that the elephant doesn't have a neck. Its head is stuck right on its body. Its mouth is under its face. Since it doesn't have a neck to stretch to the ground to eat plants, it has a trunk instead. The trunk is like a long leather pipe and is in place of a nose. An elephant drinks water with its trunk and brings grass and branches to its mouth with it. The elephant also has two long teeth that can be a yard long. They are its ivory tusks, and their value equals that of the elephant itself.

JAMILLA: An elephant is very strong and very good for riding. They put a litter, called a howdah, on its back that can carry several people. The elephant is mostly found in hot countries ...

ALI *and the villagers come out of the barn.*

JAMILLA: Looks like our teaching time is up.

LUQMAN: Thank you, I have learned so much. I look forward to the show tomorrow! Peace and blessings be on you!

BABAR and JAMILLA: And on you!

They wave good-bye, and LUQMAN *exits with the villagers. Elephant Handlers are now left alone in the courtyard.* SOPHIA *comes out of the house.*

SOPHIA: You got rid of them. If you are as good at handling gigantic beasts as well as you have handled these villagers here tonight, then tomorrow should be a good show! Tell me, how did you manage it?

BABAR: One of them had some sense. Jamilla and I spoke to him about elephants.

SOPHIA: Really? That was probably Luqman. His nose is always in a book.

ALI: That Luqman was the only one with any sense! My impatient crowd was a different story! What a joke. It was pitch dark in that barn, so they approached the animal by groping and feeling. When they reached the elephant, they had the honor of looking at it by means of touching its body. Since they hadn't seen the shape of the animal, each one has formed a different opinion about the animal's appearance!

BABAR: Well that should make for some interesting pre-show conversation.

JAMILLA: Enough of this nonsense; let's get some sleep!

All go into Sophia's house.

Scene 2. Next Day at Sophia's house.

Flags are up, and everyone is dressed up. There is a big crowd. ALI *is beating drum saying, "Come see the elephant from Hindustan!"* JAMILLA *is taking people's money as they enter.* TANGEH, PETEORPAYT, AHEER, NAK, KANN, DAND, *and* LUQMAN *come in, with crowds of people around them.* TANGEH *motions for everyone to sit down, all sit on floor.*

TANGEH: Yes, I have already seen the elephant. The Punjabis brought the elephant to me. They were going to put it on exhibit in a few days, but I saw the elephant last night.

PETEORPAYT: *(Jumps and stands up.)* I saw it too!

AHEER: *(Stands up.)* And I!

NAK: *(Stands up.)* And I!

KANN: *(Stands up.)* Me too.

DAND: *(Stands up.)* I also saw the elephant.

TANGEH: Well, yes, there were others. Let me tell you all about the elephant. It's like two columns that meet at the top. Like two strong and heavy pillars, but it is continually raising and lowering its feet. If it steps on you, you'd be crushed! *(Crowd gasps.)*

NAK: Perhaps, Brother Tangeh, that is your impression, but I found the elephant to be much more odd! It's a long animal like a snake that hangs on a tree. It bends, it straightens out. It makes a loop. It becomes a pipe. It uncoils. In short, it's completely frightening! As soon as I saw it, I got scared and stood aside! *(Sits down.)*

KANN: My knowledge of the elephant is far different. Part of the elephant is flat and soft and flexible. It moves gently, like a fan.

DAND: I must agree with Nak. The elephant is a dangerous beast. The elephant is round, hard, smooth, and very sharp at the end. It is like a spear! *(Sits down.)*

PETEORPAYT: I did a thorough investigation of the animal, and the elephant is not as remarkable as some people might lead you to believe. The elephant is like a big throne with four legs. *(Sits down.)*

AHEER: I have no knowledge of this. What I experienced of an elephant was completely different. An elephant is long and thin like a piece of rope, with a tuft like a brush at the end. *(Sits.)*

LUQMAN: *(Stands up.)* Nothing of what they are saying is true! I know what an elephant is better than they do.

PETEORPAYT: Are you calling us liars?

TANGEH: Have you seen the elephant?

LUQMAN: I haven't seen it. *(Crowd murmurs.)* I was with this group that went to visit the elephant last night, but I spoke to the elephant handlers.

NAK: You spoke to the elephant handlers?

LUQMAN: I'd read in a book that the elephant is a huge beast, but I'd never seen its picture.

KANN: You always have your nose in a book.

LUQMAN: So, when they went in to visit the elephant in the darkness, I asked the elephant keepers about it.

DAND: We had to go in the dark. It was dangerous to wake the beast.

LUQMAN: The handlers told me the elephant is very large, has a small neck, uses its trunk to stretch to the ground to eat plants and drink — and this trunk is like a water pipe. It has two long, sharp ivory teeth, and it can carry many people on its back. It's plain that my friends have each only learned about a part of the whole.

PETEORPAYT: You are calling us liars!

LUQMAN: No, it is just that you have incomplete knowledge.

JAMILLA: Now friends, patience. The elephant will appear in just a moment, and you can use your own senses and reason to make of the animal what you will!

Each person who had touched a different part of the elephant picks up a piece of the large elephant puppet. They work together to put the elephant puppet together. Once complete, BABAR *pantomimes prompting the elephant to do "Tricks."*

JAMILLA: That was the first part of our show. For the second part, for a few more pieces of silver, you and your family can ride on the back of the elephant! Line up over there for the elephant ride! *(Points off stage.* JAMILLA, ALI, *and a large part of the crowd rushes off stage.)*

TANGEH: *(Laughing.)* Well, my description of the elephant was very silly. I only felt the elephant's legs and shoulders. His legs are like tree trunks, but there is so much more to an elephant. Good for you for speaking up Luqman.

NAK: Yes, our descriptions certainly seem rather foolish now. To think I was only describing the elephant's trunk! Luqman, you were right all along.

KANN: Yes, good for you, Luqman. I was holding the elephant's ear! Next time we will know better than to pay to see something in the dark!

DAND: So much for studying elephants in the dark! I did get to feel the elephant's tusk. It's made of ivory. Ivory is rare and very expensive.

PETEORPAYT: Luqman, come over for tea this afternoon. I want to hear everything the elephant handlers told you about the elephant.

AHEER: Luqman, do you think I could take a look at your elephant books? I'd like to read it in the light. To think I was holding the elephant's tail!

They all shake his hand. Exit PETEORPAYT, AHEER, NAK, KANN, *and* DAND. TANGEH *and* LUQMAN *remain.*

TANGEH: We were all right, but we each told a different story because each one of us touched a different part of the elephant.

LUQMAN: Your palm could not grasp the whole of the beast.

TANGEH: Indeed. It never could; an elephant is much too big!

LUQMAN: It is as our beloved poet, Rumi, says, "You look at the foam ripples and not the mighty sea. We, like boats, are tossed hither and thither, We are blind though we are on the bright ocean."

The End

The Language of Animals

Based on a short story by Rumi

Cast

UNCLE CHALAQ	Pronounced "Cha-lack" (emphasis on second syllable). A man in his 40s, energetic, crafty, miserly; his name translates into "clever to the point to getting oneself into trouble" in Urdu.
SHEIKHA SHUQDA	In her 60s, wears the robes of a scholar. She is wise, gentle, gullible, and surprised when her prayers are answered.
MUSA	In his late teens, a servant to UNCLE CHALAQ. Musa is lazy by nature, but he likes to do his work quickly so he has time to loaf around. Not self-motivated.
ROOSTER	Quick and bold in his movements; likes to gossip.
DOG	Slow and deliberate in his movements; not terribly bright, always hungry.
YUNUS	A man in his 30s, suspicious, likes to gossip, nosy.
AYESHA IYAS	A young woman in her late teens or early 20s, chatty, frivolous.
IBRAHIM	Big, quick to anger, physical, generally polite but aggressive when provoked.

Production Notes:

Setting: A village with at least four different doors. Uncle Chalaq's house must have a common room/bedroom and an outdoor courtyard.

Scene 1. In front of SHEIKHA SHUQDA's house.

SHEIKHA SHUQDA *and* UNCLE CHALAQ *are seated and drinking tea together.*

UNCLE CHALAQ: O Sheikha Shuqda, I have listened to you for many years, but I haven't gotten any benefit from your teachings.

SHEIKHA SHUQDA: Is that so?

UNCLE CHALAQ: Nevertheless, I think I deserve something for my patience in listening to you, so I've come to you today with a request.

SHEIKHA SHUQDA: Tell me what your request is, and if I can, I'll do it.

UNCLE CHALAQ: I want you to pray for me and ask our Creator to teach me the language of animals. I want to learn valuable lessons from their conversations.

SHEIKHA SHUQDA: The language of animals?

UNCLE CHALAQ: Yes.

SHEIKHA SHUQDA: I don't want to throw a wet blanket on your plans, but I don't think this would be advisable for you.

UNCLE CHALAQ: Why not?

SHEIKHA SHUQDA: You can learn as much as you need from your own experience and the experiences of your friends …

UNCLE CHALAQ: *(Interrupting.)* My friends mostly talk nonsense.

SHEIKHA SHUQDA: You can also learn from books and the lives of others.

UNCLE CHALAQ: I'm a very busy man, and I don't have time to read. Besides, books are expensive.

SHEIKHA SHUQDA: Let me understand: You feel that you have learned everything there is to be learned from experience, books, and friends, so that now all that is left is the language of animals?

UNCLE CHALAQ: That about sums it up.

Uncomfortable silence as SHEIKHA SHUQDA *strokes her chin and contemplates* UNCLE CHALAQ*'s answers.*

UNCLE CHALAQ: Look Sheikha, I really think those animals know how to worship God in a very simple and sincere way. I could benefit from their example.

SHEIKHA SHUQDA: In our tradition, you must first go and learn as much as you can using your own human language, and that alone should be enough for 70 generations! As for learning the language of animals, that's just a whim and idle longing. Too much of that brings trouble to a man.

UNCLE CHALAQ: I don't want trouble. I want to understand new things from a different perspective. I have a dog that guards my house. I have chickens and donkeys and sheep. I am surrounded by animals every single day, but I don't know a thing they are talking about. If I understand my neighbors, then I will be able to improve my own character.

SHEIKHA SHUQDA: Very well, you want to know what they are saying. I want to know many things too, but when it isn't right, when it isn't the right time, then it's better not to know.

UNCLE CHALAQ: Aren't you always telling us to seek knowledge?

SHEIKHA SHUQDA: Listen to me. There are better ways to seek knowledge that are not so dangerous. Put away this fancy idea and go back to your normal work. Don't think too much about being clever, for too much cleverness may bring with it much woe.

UNCLE CHALAQ: *(Chuckling.)* Woe?

SHEIKHA SHUQDA: Responsibility is perhaps a better word. With knowledge comes responsibility, and I'm not sure you're ready for it.

UNCLE CHALAQ: I am ready, and I can't give up. I've got to learn the language of animals. I'll accept the danger and responsibility. You are a generous person. Please pray for me. I'm just asking for the ability to understand the language of chickens and dogs. I'll be satisfied if I learn just those two: chickens and dogs.

SHEIKHA SHUQDA: Very well. *(Sighs.)* As long as you are willing to accept the responsibility it may bring.

UNCLE CHALAQ *nods head vigorously.*

SHEIKHA SHUQDA: I'll pray that you may understand the language of chickens and dogs. But I'm not responsible if you lose by it.

UNCLE CHALAQ: Oh no, dear Sheikha! You will see!

Lights dim.

Scene 2. UNCLE CHALAQ*'s bedroom, early morning.*

A rooster is heard crowing. Uncle Chalaq wakes up, stretches, and rings a bell next to his bed. MUSA *enters.*

UNCLE CHALAQ: Bring me breakfast, and let the dog and rooster come in.

MUSA: Come in here? To your room?

UNCLE CHALAQ: Yes, my room. Let them in. I desire their company.

MUSA *shrugs and exits.*

Enter MUSA *with tray,* DOG, *and* ROOSTER. MUSA *sets the tray down on table.* ROOSTER *perches on chair;* DOG *flops on ground.* UNCLE CHALAQ *starts to eat his breakfast, and a piece of bread falls on the ground.* ROOSTER *swoops down and grabs it before* DOG.

DOG: What a rotten rooster you are.

UNCLE CHALAQ *stares at* DOG, *catches himself, and pretends not to notice the dog. However, he is smiling profusely because he now understands their language.*

DOG: *(To* ROOSTER.*)* You eat wheat. You eat millet. You eat barley. You eat flies.

ROOSTER: Those are hard to catch!

DOG: You eat cockroaches.

ROOSTER: Love that texture; crunchy.

DOG: You hunt in the garden and eat earthworms and a thousand other things.

ROOSTER: Can I help it if I'm talented?

DOG: You know that I can't get anything other than that bread. Yet you wouldn't even let me eat that one breadcrumb!

ROOSTER: Don't be mad. Later today, something will happen to make you very happy. Everyone knows that meat is tastier than anything else to you; much better than bread.

DOG: So?

ROOSTER: In a few hours, the master's horse will fall dead, and you'll be able to eat as much meat as you want.

DOG: I'd forgotten all about that. As long as this is the way things will be, why then, you eat the bread! Enjoy your meal!

UNCLE CHALAQ: Musa! I'm finished with my breakfast. Take my tray away, and put these animals back into the yard.

MUSA *enters, takes tray, and herds animals away. Exit* MUSA, DOG, *and* ROOSTER.

UNCLE CHALAQ: Incredible! The horse is going to die this morning? It's a good thing that I found this out. Learning the language of animals is as useful as I suspected it would be. Useful and lucrative! *(Rubbing his index finger and thumb together as though polishing a coin.)* Heh heh heh. Musa! Musa come here!

MUSA *enters.*

UNCLE CHALAQ: Take that horse to the market as fast as you can and sell it for whatever it will bring.

MUSA: What? That is your only horse.

UNCLE CHALAQ: Who is in charge around here? Do as I say.

MUSA: Very well, sir. Sell your only horse at the market.

MUSA *exits room.* UNCLE CHALAQ *gets dressed and goes outside to* DOG *and* ROOSTER. MUSA *comes back with a small sack of coins, gives the bag to* UNCLE CHALAQ *and exits.* UNCLE CHALAQ *counts out coins, goes back into his house, and stuffs the coins under his mattress.* UNCLE CHALAQ *goes back into the yard with* DOG *and* ROOSTER.

DOG: Hey Rooster, you said that the horse was going to die this morning, but it didn't happen. The master sold it. What am I going to do for food?

ROOSTER: I didn't lie. The horse was supposed to die, but the master sold it, and *(looks up at the sky in one corner)* according to those sparrows, the horse has died in the stable of the man who bought it. But since it was ordained that the master must suffer some loss and it didn't happen, then this afternoon his donkey will die.

DOG: The donkey? But I just saw him this morning.

ROOSTER: Hey, the death of a donkey is like a wedding feast for a dog.

DOG: *(Sadly.)* True, true.

ROOSTER: For supper, you'll eat meat, but I won't as I can't eat meat.

DOG: No meat for you; donkey meat for me.

UNCLE CHALAQ: Musa! Musa! Come here at once!

MUSA *enters.*

MUSA: What is it Master?

UNCLE CHALAQ: I want you to take the donkey immediately to market and sell it for whatever price you can get.

MUSA: But Master, we just sold the horse, and we need the donkey to …

UNCLE CHALAQ: *(Interrupts.)* Who is in charge around here?

MUSA: You are.

UNCLE CHALAQ: Then do as I say.

MUSA: But Master, the big donkey market isn't until next week. I'm not going to get a very good price if I sell it today.

UNCLE CHALAQ: Did I ask you about next week? No! I asked you about today; now go immediately and sell that donkey. Take whatever you can get for it.

MUSA: As you say, Master. *(To himself.)* What has gotten into him? Normally he haggles over everything, even the price of the smallest onion, and now he wants me to practically give these animals away. *(Shakes his head.)*

MUSA *exits.*

UNCLE CHALAQ: Knowing this language of the animals is very handy indeed!

Lights dim.

Scene 3. UNCLE CHALAQ*'s bedroom the next morning.*

ROOSTER *crows offstage.* UNCLE CHALAQ *wakes up, stretches, and rings bell. After a few moments,* MUSA *knocks on door with breakfast tray.* MUSA *enters.*

MUSA: Morning, sir.

UNCLE CHALAQ: Ah Musa, excellent work with those sales yesterday. Now please, bring in the rooster and dog.

MUSA: *(Looking surprised.)* The rooster and dog? Again? *(*UNCLE CHALAQ *nods head.)* As you wish, sir.

MUSA *exits.* UNCLE CHALAQ *eats his breakfast.*

Enter MUSA, DOG, *and* ROOSTER. ROOSTER *perches on chair.* DOG *flops on ground. Exit* MUSA. *As* UNCLE CHALAQ *eats, a slice of bread falls on the ground.* ROOSTER *swoops down and grabs the bread before* DOG *has a chance to get it.*

DOG: Hey there! Your promises make me feel good, but at the end of the day, you go back on your word and there is no meat!

ROOSTER: What are you talking about, dear friend?

DOG: You've already forgotten about yesterday.

ROOSTER: Sorry, I'm drawing a blank here.

DOG: The morning when the master's horse was supposed to die but he sold it instead?

ROOSTER: Ah yes. Poor dead horse.

DOG: That died in someone else's barn. And then when I had hopes of eating the donkey meat in the afternoon, he sold the donkey!

ROOSTER: Ah, yes. Poor dead donkey.

DOG: Dead in someone else's barn! If that's the way it is to be, you shouldn't eat the bread at breakfast. After all, I have some rights in this household, too!

ROOSTER: You have rights; I don't argue with you on that. But I don't understand how the master has suddenly become so smart.

DOG: Yes, this is quite surprising.

ROOSTER: He can fend off any loss. However, anything that has a substitute is no cause for complaint. This morning at dawn while I was crowing, I heard that in place of the horse and donkey that the master has sold, four of his black sheep will die.

DOG: Four sheep?

ROOSTER: Yes, all four.

DOG: How delicious — I mean tragic.

ROOSTER: Well, when they die, the bodies will be taken and thrown away in the desert, as carrion meat is unlawful for people to eat. Then you can go to the desert and eat as much as you want! It's not against dog laws!

DOG: I know about those rules. Poor master; one can't prevent all loss. The horse was sold, and the donkey was sold. In their place, the black sheep will die. Fine. I'll be patient.

UNCLE CHALAQ: Musa! Musa! Take away my tray. Get rid of these animals! Take them out to the yard. Go! Go! (*Animals stand up.* MUSA *enters and herds them out. Exit* MUSA, DOG, *and* ROOSTER.)

UNCLE CHALAQ: Musa! Musa! Get back in here.

MUSA *enters, breathless.*

UNCLE CHALAQ: I want you to take the four black sheep to the market and sell them. Not the white sheep.

MUSA: Not the white sheep.

UNCLE CHALAQ: Not the brown sheep.

MUSA: Not the brown sheep.

UNCLE CHALAQ: Sell all four black sheep.

MUSA: Sell all the black sheep.

UNCLE CHALAQ: Sell the black sheep. Take any price you can get.

MUSA: Four black sheep, as you say.

Exit MUSA.

UNCLE CHALAQ: The knowledge of the language of the animals is indeed very profitable! *(He starts to dance around.)* I've prevented loss from my own property after learning the speech of dogs and chickens. I've gained some gold and sold my loss!

Scene 4. UNCLE CHALAQ's courtyard and greater village, some time just after noon.

UNCLE CHALAQ *enters courtyard dressed in fancy clothes. Dog and* ROOSTER *are in yard.* MUSA *enters, breathless, with small sack of coins, and hands the bag to* UNCLE CHALAQ. UNCLE CHALAQ *slaps hands together, starts to count out the coins.*

UNCLE CHALAQ: Musa, good job. Now go prepare my lunch.

MUSA *exits*.

DOG: Lunch? Lunch! Now it is my turn, Rooster. I know what was supposed to happen, but it all turned out differently. The horse was sold, the donkey was sold, and even the sheep were sold!

ROOSTER: Yes, there does seem to be a seller's market around here.

DOG: I can't stay hungry forever. Our master is very clever.

ROOSTER: A little too clever.

DOG: Whatever loss there is supposed to be, he prevents it!

ROOSTER: The master's cleverness won't last much longer. Too much shrewdness ends badly. The master himself will die today!

DOG: But he looks so healthy?

ROOSTER: Well, he's a goner. And once that happens, then his family and relatives will give alms. They'll distribute bread, they'll cook up a big pot of stew, and give everyone a bowlful.

DOG: Ah yes, the funeral spread.

ROOSTER: They'll slaughter sheep. There will be much to enjoy, and you'll have your portion, my friend.

DOG: How do you know he'll die today?

ROOSTER: I heard it from the birds in the field. Our master wasn't supposed to die this soon, but he has acquired some things unlawfully. The neighbor's parrot was telling me that when a person's blood is diseased, leeches are applied to suck out the bad blood.

DOG: The master needs leeches?

ROOSTER: No. He was supposed to suffer some losses to compensate for his past bad behavior.

DOG: What kind of losses are you talking about? Blood?

ROOSTER: No! Loss of his property in the form of his animals. His horse was to die, but the clever man sold it. Then in place of that, the donkey was supposed to die, but the master sold the donkey too. Then the four sheep were supposed to die, but he prevented any loss to himself from that. The death of these animals was supposed to compensate for the bad things he does to his soul.

DOG: And provide my lunch.

ROOSTER: Since he didn't allow those losses to happen, now the calamity will fall on his own neck. He cannot sell that.

DOG: These rules of fate are very complicated.

ROOSTER: Yes. Just remember: Too much cleverness can be the cause of a disaster, even death!

UNCLE CHALAQ *trembles with terror and runs to* SHEIKHA SHUQDA's *house. He bangs on the Sheikha's door.*

UNCLE CHALAQ: O wise Sheikha! O kind Sheikha Shuqda, please let me in! Please help me!

SHEIKHA SHUQDA: Peace be upon you brother. What is wrong? Calm yourself.

UNCLE CHALAQ: O please dear Sheikha, you must help me! I am ruined.

SHEIKHA SHUQDA: What has happened? What are you afraid of?

UNCLE CHALAQ: I am certain that something awful will happen to me. I listened to my dog and rooster.

SHEIKHA SHUQDA: You listened to … So it actually worked? My prayer worked?

UNCLE CHALAQ: Yes!

SHEIKHA SHUQDA: You understand the language of animals?

UNCLE CHALAQ: Yes! Yes! Yes! Well, actually just dogs and roosters. But that has gotten me into enough trouble.

SHEIKHA SHUQDA: I don't understand.

UNCLE CHALAQ: The rooster and dog told me my livestock would die …my horse, then my donkey, and four black sheep. Acting on their advice, I sold all the beasts before they could die.

SHEIKHA SHUQDA: You sold the animals to someone else knowing they would die? Did you tell the buyer about the risk?

UNCLE CHALAQ: Of course not! I wanted to pass my loss to someone else. I did, and got gold in return.

SHEIKHA SHUQDA: I warned you that learning the language of animals would bring you no good.

UNCLE CHALAQ: I couldn't see that at the time; I could only see the gold. But now this rooster says that I must die to compensate for the bad things I've done to my soul. My soul? What can I do? I'm too young to die!

SHEIKHA SHUQDA: It must be like the poet Rumi says: "The sight which regards the ebb and flow of good and ill opens a passage for you from misfortune to happiness. Thence you see the one state moves you into the other, one opposite state generating its opposite in exchange."

UNCLE CHALAQ: I don't have time for poetry or philosophy! I'm going to die! I need help.

SHEIKHA SHUQDA: My poor fellow, there is nothing I can do. I have no power over life and death. So these animals predicted you would suffer some losses with regard to your livestock?

UNCLE CHALAQ: Yes, but I prevented the losses by selling the doomed animals.

SHEIKHA SHUQDA: Those losses were actually meant to stop further calamity from happening to you. You told me you wanted to improve your character, but instead I see you sold your horse, donkey, and sheep and bought trouble for yourself.

UNCLE CHALAQ: Trouble, yes, and gold. O Sheikha, is there is nothing you can do?

SHEIKHA SHUQDA: There can be no cheating in the works of fate. I am powerless.

UNCLE CHALAQ: I'm begging you. Please tell me what I should do.

SHEIKHA SHUQDA: Weren't the horse, the donkey, and the sheep supposed to be alms to protect your life?

UNCLE CHALAQ: I don't know about that. (SHEIKHA SHUQDA *looks at him sternly.*) Um, yes. They were supposed to die so I would be spared.

SHEIKHA SHUQDA: Try going to the people who bought the animals and suffered the loss that you were supposed to take. Ask for their forgiveness. Perhaps if you return the money to at least one of them, then you will take the loss upon yourself.

UNCLE CHALAQ: I have to give up some of my gold?

SHEIKHA SHUQDA: If one of them agrees to a refund, perhaps your fate will be altered.

UNCLE CHALAQ: You may be on to something! I'll go right away and fix things. Refunds for everyone! Peace and blessings be upon you!

SHEIKHA SHUQDA: And on you also. *(She closes her door.)*

UNCLE CHALAQ *runs back towards his house and stops as he comes upon* MUSA.

UNCLE CHALAQ: Musa, whom did you sell the sheep to?

MUSA: I sold them to Yunus.

UNCLE CHALAQ: Yunus? Excellent! Now there is a man who knows how to carry a grudge. He'll want five times what he paid for those sheep as a refund. I'm saved!

UNCLE CHALAQ *goes to the house of* YUNUS *and bangs on the door.* YUNUS *opens door.*

UNCLE CHALAQ: Peace be upon you.

YUNUS: And on you.

UNCLE CHALAQ: Yunus, were you the one who bought four sickly black sheep this morning?

YUNUS: Yes. And it's a good thing that I did, because all four of them died a few hours after I bought them.

UNCLE CHALAQ: No! It was very bad. You must feel very upset and angry.

YUNUS: No, actually, I'm not mad at all.

UNCLE CHALAQ: I'll bet you have a big grudge right now.

YUNUS: Grudge? No, can't say that I do.

UNCLE CHALAQ: No need to waste any more time on angry feelings. You've suffered a loss, and I've come to make it up to you.

YUNUS: Make it up to me?

UNCLE CHALAQ: I want to return your money to you, and I want you to excuse me, because I knew the animals were sick when I sold them.

YUNUS: You knew they were sick? But you never said anything to me.

UNCLE CHALAQ: I am very sorry for what I did. Here is your refund! *(He shoves a purse of money into* YUNUS' *hands.* YUNUS *shoves the money back at him.)*

YUNUS: I don't want your refund. I'm very happy with the way things turned out.

UNCLE CHALAQ: How can you possibly be happy? *(He shoves a purse of money into* YUNUS' *hands.* YUNUS *shoves the money back at him.)*

YUNUS: Do you know that I had a lawsuit against somebody?

UNCLE CHALAQ: No I didn't, but you are often at court.

YUNUS: I wanted to take the four sheep to the judge's house and give them as a bribe so that he would issue a verdict in my favor. But since the sheep died this very morning, I wasn't able to do that!

UNCLE CHALAQ: *(Shoves the money bag into* YUNUS' *hand.)* Take the money and get more sheep.

YUNUS: *(Shoves the money back to* UNCLE CHALAQ.*)* You don't understand. I don't want more sheep.

UNCLE CHALAQ: You need the sheep to bribe the judge and win your case.

YUNUS: I heard just now that the judge had ordered that if anyone brings a bribe to his house, that person will be thrown in prison. The judge said anyone who tries to give a bribe wants to pervert truth, and for that crime he should be punished.

UNCLE CHALAQ: More philosophy? Forget the legal proceedings; you lost money. *(He tries to shove money to* YUNUS. YUNUS *pushes it back.)*

YUNUS: It was a good thing that the sheep died! If they hadn't, I'd be in prison right now. I am thankful that a small loss saved me from a greater catastrophe. That's why the purchase was a good deal! The money is yours. I've learned a lesson worth more than a hundred sheep and a thousand pieces of silver. Thank you Uncle Chalaq, thank you! You have taught me well. You have taught me so, so, so well. *(*YUNUS *shakes his hand and closes the door.)*

UNCLE CHALAQ: Yes, wonderful for you. My favorite student.

He leaves dejected, walking toward home. Enter MUSA, *strolling.*

UNCLE CHALAQ: Musa! Musa! Whom did you sell the donkey to?

MUSA: To Ayesha Iyas.

UNCLE CHALAQ: Ayesha Iyas? What's she like?

MUSA: Oh, she is one of these girls who always must be doing what her friends are doing. She buys what they buy, eats what they eat, wears what they wear, talks how they talk. You know the type.

UNCLE CHALAQ: Were people buying a lot of donkeys that day?

MUSA: No, that is why I didn't get a very good price for the animal.

UNCLE CHALAQ: Perhaps this dead donkey prevented her from having fun with her friends. She'll be angry and disappointed. And surely she'll want the money to get a new donkey and keep up with her friends! Yes!

UNCLE CHALAQ *goes to Ayesha Iyas' house. Knocks on door.* AYESHA IYAS *opens the door.*

UNCLE CHALAQ: Peace be upon you Sister Ayesha Iyas.

AYESHA IYAS: And on you Uncle Chalaq.

UNCLE CHALAQ: Sister Ayesha, did you buy a donkey yesterday?

AYESHA IYAS: Yes, and it's a very good thing that I did, because the donkey died the same day!

UNCLE CHALAQ: Oh no. The donkey died? You must be exceptionally disappointed. You've suffered a loss, and I've come now to make it up to you. That donkey was mine, and I knew it was about to die. Now I want to return your money and get your forgiveness. Here is your full refund. *(Holds up money bag.)*

AYESHA IYAS: I don't want a refund.

UNCLE CHALAQ: Why on earth not?

AYESHA IYAS: I'm very satisfied with the way things turned out. Do you know why I bought that donkey?

UNCLE CHALAQ: I have no idea.

AYESHA IYAS: I bought it because I was very unhappy that I didn't own a donkey. Some of my friends had donkeys, and they had decided to ride them to a certain village last night. Since I didn't have a donkey, I wouldn't have been able to go with them. I was very upset about that until yesterday, when I bought your donkey.

UNCLE CHALAQ: But then the donkey died; you couldn't meet your friends. How sad.

AYESHA IYAS: Well, yes, at the time, I was very disappointed.

UNCLE CHALAQ: Ah! Disappointed! I have just the cure for disappointment: Gold!

AYESHA IYAS: But I'm not disappointed anymore.

UNCLE CHALAQ: Why on earth not? You missed the donkey trip to the village.

AYESHA IYAS: You don't understand. My friends did leave without me. As they were crossing some open land, they met a pack of rabid wolves. The wolves tore their donkeys to pieces and bit them badly. They are still in the hospital.

UNCLE CHALAQ: Rabid wolves?

AYESHA IYAS: When I heard that, I was thankful that my donkey had died and averted the calamity from my neck. If not, I would now be lying in the hospital, too. If I had bought a different donkey, a healthy one, I would have gone with them and suffered their fate. *(Smiling.)* So for this reason, I am happy and satisfied with the deal. I don't want your money. Indeed, if you wish, please let me give you more money for the donkey! One moment, let me get you some coins.

UNCLE CHALAQ: No! No! *(As* AYESHA *goes back inside,* UNCLE CHALAQ *runs away).* Musa! Musa!

MUSA *enters*.

MUSA: Yes, master.

UNCLE CHALAQ: Musa, this is very, very important. To whom did you sell the horse? Think lad.

MUSA: I sold the horse to Ibrahim.

UNCLE CHALAQ: *(Relieved.)* Excellent. Ibrahim has a horrible temper. He'll be very angry about this dead horse. Why, I bet he'll probably beat me before I even have time to offer him the refund.

MUSA: Do you want me to go with you, for protection?

UNCLE CHALAQ: Of course not! Maybe if I'm lucky, he'll knock out some of my teeth or break a bone — all that ought to save me!

MUSA: As you wish, master.

MUSA *exits.* UNCLE CHALAQ *goes to* IBRAHIM*'s house and knocks on door.*

UNCLE CHALAQ: Peace be upon you, Brother Ibrahim.

IBRAHIM: And on you, Uncle Chalaq. To what do I owe this visit?

UNCLE CHALAQ: Ibrahim, did you buy a horse on the point of death yesterday?

IBRAHIM: Yes, I did, and it's a good thing that I did buy it, because the horse died later that morning.

UNCLE CHALAQ: I think that is called a bad thing.

IBRAHIM: What nonsense are you spouting?

UNCLE CHALAQ: That horse was mine, and I knew that it was about to die. Now I've come to give you a refund. I want to give you your money back so that you will be happy.

IBRAHIM: I don't want your money.

UNCLE CHALAQ: My dear Brother Ibrahim, let's be very clear here. You suffered grave financial loss. You must be quite angry.

IBRAHIM: Actually, no, I'm not. That horse was very beneficial for me, and I'm quite satisfied with things the way they are.

UNCLE CHALAQ: This is unbelievable.

IBRAHIM: You see, I was planning to travel on some business to a distant village. The day before I bought your horse, I found a traveler going to the same village as me. He had a horse, and I said to myself that I should buy a horse so that I could go with him. I went to the market and bought your horse because it was, by far, the cheapest horse in the entire town. A little while later after I purchased it, the beast neighed and fell down stone dead.

At first I was very unhappy about that, and I was forced to postpone my trip.

UNCLE CHALAQ: Yes, this is what I'm talking about. Postponing trip, loss of the horse, double loss because you might have made so much money on that business trip!

IBRAHIM: It didn't turn out that way. Later, I learned that the man I was planning to travel with went anyway and ran into some highwaymen in the desert. They stole his horse and nearly beat him to death.

UNCLE CHALAQ: But, but …

IBRAHIM: That's why I am thankful that the death of the horse prevented me from going on that journey. Otherwise, I would have lost the horse, and Lord knows what would have happened to me at the hands of those brigands. I am very satisfied with the loss that saved me from a greater trouble.

UNCLE CHALAQ: *(Pleading.)* Dear friend. Now that things are right with you, come and take back your money. I am sorry that I sold you that dying horse. I'm in deep trouble now, and only you can save me.

IBRAHIM: Since you knew that horse had a defect and you sold it anyway, I'm not about to do business with you.

UNCLE CHALAQ: What?

IBRAHIM: How do I know that there is not another trick in your wanting to give back the money? Whatever it may be, go think of something else. I'm not interested in your money. I am satisfied with the deal that we made, and there is no reason to take your money for nothing.

UNCLE CHALAQ: No, please! You must, you must. *(He grabs* IBRAHIM*'s arm.)* I'm too young to die!

IBRAHIM: *(Shakes him off his arm, and* UNCLE CHALAQ *falls to the ground in a heap.)* Away with you! *(Slams door.)*

UNCLE CHALAQ: *(Dejected. Walks toward his house.)* I'll return to Sheikha Shuqda and perhaps she'll have another plan for me. These people who don't know the language of animals are smarter than I am, and I should have learned from their actions. I wish that I had never learned the language of animals!

UNCLE CHALAQ *is now in front of his courtyard, and* UNCLE CHALAQ *sees* ROOSTER *and* DOG. UNCLE CHALAQ *points to* ROOSTER.

UNCLE CHALAQ: Rooster! You have brought nothing but ruin upon me. I've been feeding you your entire life. What business did you have with predicting the future?

ROOSTER: *(Surprised.)* I was minding my own business. What business do you have with the language of animals when you couldn't learn from the language of people?

At this moment, UNCLE CHALAQ *falls to the ground dead.* DOG *and* ROOSTER *go over and sniff at dead body and test him to see that he is dead. They take a few steps back from the body.*

ROOSTER: *(Looks at* DOG.*)* Are you still hungry?

The End

Alternate ending:

DOG *sniffs at* UNCLE CHALAQ*'s body.* DOG *slowly starts to take a bite of* UNCLE CHALAQ*'s hand, when* UNCLE CHALAQ *bolts upright, shaking his hand.* ROOSTER *and* DOG *jump back in horror and surprise.* UNCLE CHALAQ *uses* DOG*'s body to help him stand upright.*

UNCLE CHALAQ: *(To audience.)* I've been given a second chance! *(He draws a moneybag out of his shirt pocket.)* The first thing I am going to do is buy my dog a proper lunch!

The End

Destiny at Sea

Based on a short story by Saadi

Cast
CLOTH TRADER   In his 40s, confident, a bit superstitious.

BRASS TRADER   In his 50s, nervous because his inventory will be lost if the boat sinks.

BOOKISH MAN   In his 30s, self-assured, school teacher, talkative, wears Western clothes, charismatic, likes to be the center of attention.

BOOKISH WOMAN   In her 20s, Bookish Man's wife, a schoolteacher, wears Western clothes, knows how to give her husband center stage.

SAILOR   In his 20s, open, honest, common sense.

TWO DECKHANDS

RESCUED FISHERMAN

Production Notes:

Transform the theater into the ocean by having stagehands stand in the theater aisles holding long bolts of blue cloth at the top and bottom of the aisles. When the storm comes, they shake the cloth to make rough "waves."

Setting: On the deck of a large boat.

Onstage are CLOTH TRADER *and* BRASS TRADER, *with samples of their wares, as well as* BOOKISH MAN *and* BOOKISH WOMAN *with a picnic basket, small suitcase, and lots of books.* DECKHANDS *and* SAILOR *enter, walk back and forth across ship, getting it ready, then exit. After adjusting their wares/basket, the passengers look into the audience/at the ocean.*

BOOKISH MAN: Look how far we have gone. The coast is growing smaller and smaller.

BOOKISH WOMAN: We are surrounded. "Water, water everywhere, and all the boards did shrink; Water, water everywhere, nor any drop to drink!"

BOOKISH MAN: "Roll on thou deep and dark blue ocean — roll! Ten thousand fleets sweep over thee in vain; Man marks the earth with his ruin, his control stops with thy shore ..." Perhaps! *(The couple laughs together.)*

BRASS TRADER: "Rahega Raawi, wo Neel wo Fraat mey kabbthak? Thera safina key hey bahrey bey karaan key liyay." Whether you travel on the River Ravi, or Nile, or Euphrates, your ship was made to sail on a limitless ocean.

BOOKISH WOMAN: *(Claps her hands together and holds them over her heart.)* Why that's just lovely.

All nod approvingly.

BOOKISH MAN: That couplet: Did Allama Mohammad Iqbal write it?

BRASS TRADER *nods.*

CLOTH TRADER: "A sign for them is that We carried their offspring in a laden boat. And We have created for them of its like that they ride. And if We will, We may drown them. There will be none to whom they cry aloud for help, nor will they be saved unless it be a mercy from Us and as an enjoyment for a while."

BOOKISH MAN: *(Thoughtfully.)* The noble Quran.

All nod solemnly.

BRASS TRADER: *(Claps one hand on Bookish Man's shoulder and then points out to sea with the other hand.)* See that small sailboat? They shouldn't be setting out in the open sea in such a tiny boat.

BOOKISH WOMAN: If a storm breaks, they'll be in a lot of danger.

CLOTH TRADER: But as you said so before brother: "If We will, We may drown them." I believe in destiny. The will of man is an empty fantasy.

BOOKISH WOMAN: You believe in absolute predestination? (CLOTH TRADER *looks at her not understanding.*) Predestination, fate, destiny: Everything is determined beforehand?

CLOTH TRADER: Yes! Absolutely! No escaping destiny!

BOOKISH MAN: On the contrary my good man; Man's fate is the result of his intelligence, his knowledge, and education.

BRASS TRADER: No, no, no, brother, the accounting of fate is not in our hands. No one knows anything. Who is to say that our ship will reach its destination safely and the little boat will not?

BOOKISH MAN: There is a big difference between our big ship and that tiny sailboat. It's true that no man knows everything, but he must take control of his affairs as much as he is able and make sensible choices. Drifting thoughtlessly in small boats may be a relaxing caprice, but in the end, it can only lead to failure.

BOOKISH WOMAN: You ought to be more respectful of those men in that small boat. *(Squinting at boat.)* I think they are fishermen. Look, every person has his own job. One is a trader who buys and sells. Another is a scholar who follows his researches and enquires. The men in that small boat are probably poor fishermen. They can't afford a big boat, but sometimes one must take risks for greater rewards.

BOOKISH MAN: I suppose you are right, my dear.

BOOKISH WOMAN: If everyone were afraid of the ocean and remained at home, then the world's trade would collapse.

BOOKISH MAN: Nonsense, there are still the land routes. (BOOKISH WOMAN *starts to pout.)* Certainly one must look for the best way to do anything. When going out to sea, you have to choose the best ship, and that's what we have done.

BRASS TRADER: A person who travels over water should know how to swim.

CLOTH TRADER: God forgive your father! If there is a storm and the ship breaks in the middle of the ocean, what good will your swimming do?

BOOKISH MAN: Ah, but you speak from your inexperience. Knowing something is always better than not knowing something. A person who doesn't know how to swim can drown taking a bath! The person who knows how to swim may be able to keep afloat until some means of help arrives.

BRASS TRADER: That's what I've been saying. But a passenger in a small boat should stay near the coast, even if he knows how to swim.

CLOTH TRADER: I was saying something else. I'm talking about destiny! It doesn't make any difference if you're near the coast or far away from it. If your life is not over, you'll survive a raging inferno or the ocean's waves. If not, you won't survive even in your own bed at home. Destiny, my friends, destiny.

BOOKISH MAN: No dear friend, don't speak like that!

BOOKISH WOMAN: Your life is over; your life is not over. What does that mean? The accounting of a man's life is not in the hands of blind and deaf destiny. A person's destiny is made by himself.

BOOKISH MAN: If a man walks into a raging inferno without wearing protective clothing, he will certainly burn. If the life of a person were entirely a matter of predestination and destiny, no one would bother to take any precautions for his own safety.

BOOKISH WOMAN: I myself am fearful right now for the destiny of those people in that small boat.

BOOKISH MAN: Don't waste your fears. How do we know they aren't expert swimmers?

BOOKISH WOMAN: It's said that even a mad man is aware of his own best interest.

BOOKISH MAN: Anyway, why should there be a storm?

BRASS TRADER: Well, they've taken care to follow our big ship, haven't they? If they have a problem, they can reach us.

BOOKISH WOMAN: That's just talk! God forbid that something bad should happen.

CLOTH TRADER: Who knows what may happen?

BRASS TRADER: It's smart for everyone to consider what might happen before it happens.

BOOKISH MAN: There is a saying: "A problem should be solved before it occurs."

BRASS TRADER: Now that's what I'm talking about. Life is not without calculation! We who are traders, if we were to think that all we have to do is depend on destiny for our livelihood and not use our brains, well, we might as well carry cumin seed to Kerman to sell. (*Everyone stares at him blankly.*) That is where cumin seeds come from! *(Everyone nods.)*

CLOTH TRADER: We would surely lose our money if we sold cumin in Kerman.

BRASS TRADER: Only fools set out without using their heads.

A strong wind begins to blow. The ship starts to rock. DECKHANDS *and* SAILOR *enter and tie things down, exit again; merchants and travelers hold onto their baggage and each other tightly. The rocking gets stronger; the passengers hold onto anything they can find.* SAILOR *enters to strike the sails.*

BOOKISH MAN: A big wave has crashed over the little boat and turned it over! Two men have fallen into the water!

BOOKISH WOMAN: The storm is pushing their boat away from them!

BRASS TRADER: Now they'll drown! If any of you can do something, if anyone can save those two men, I'll give him 100 gold coins as a reward, 50 for each one who is saved!

SAILOR: I can do it. Nobody else but me can survive those waves.

He dives into the water, i.e. one of the aisles. Exits via the back theater doors. Big ship is still rocking.

BOOKISH MAN: He is swimming toward the men! He has one of the men.

BOOKISH WOMAN: The other man has disappeared beneath the waves.

BOOKISH MAN: Everything is just as I said. Now you see.

The rocking of the ship subsides. Enter SAILOR *and* RESCUED FISHERMAN. *They come aboard the ship.* RESCUED FISHERMAN *is wrapped in blankets by* DECKHANDS, *and they exit stage.* SAILOR *rests on ship, exhausted, waiting for his money.* BRASS TRADER *gives* SAILOR *a small purse.* SAILOR *opens purse and starts counting out coins.*

CLOTH TRADER: This is exactly what we have been talking about. The destined life of one of them was over and he drowned, but the other still has life remaining, so he was saved. No one knows anything. Every person has his own destiny.

BOOKISH MAN: No, it was just as I said. Who is now receiving the reward of 50 gold coins? The man who knew how to swim!

BOOKISH WOMAN: The one who took the biggest risk.

BOOKISH MAN: No one else earned anything in the middle of this sea. The young sailor made an effort and learned how to swim. Today he has been rewarded for his efforts!

BRASS TRADER: No, it's just as I said. I told you I was afraid from the beginning. Now did you see how that other man was drowned?

SAILOR: It's true that the sea is full of danger, and there are many unexpected things that happen in life. But there is also another consideration.

BOOKISH WOMAN: Another consideration?

BOOKISH MAN: I think we have covered everything — destiny, calculated risk, and free will.

SAILOR: I got the reward because I knew how to swim. Do any of you know how to swim?

Everyone looks down and silently nods or mumbles "No."

47

SAILOR: I thought as much. It is the wages of knowledge and the hire of skill. If someone else had been able to help, then we could have saved both men. I wasn't able to bring them both back to the ship by myself. If I had tried to take them both, they would have overpowered me in their panic, and things would have become very difficult. We all might have drowned together.

CLOTH TRADER: Only one could be saved.

BRASS TRADER: Calculated risk.

SAILOR: They were in fact two brothers from my neighborhood, and I knew them both.

BOOKISH WOMAN: You knew those men in that little boat?

SAILOR: Yes, as I was jumping into the water, everything came back to me. When we were children, one of them once hit me unfairly while we were playing. But the other, when he found me one day in the desert tired and weak, let me ride his camel home. They themselves had settled their destiny long ago!

BOOKISH MAN: How is that possible?

SAILOR: I was able to save only one of them today, so I chose the one whom I like and went to his side. Anyone in my place would have done the same. He would first save the person who had done him a kindness. And that is what I did.

All the passengers are silent and pondering for a moment.

CLOTH TRADER: If he hadn't known them, the choice wouldn't have mattered.

BOOKISH WOMAN: If they hadn't found themselves in the middle of the sea, one of them wouldn't have been drowned.

BRASS TRADER: If they had been far from our ship, even that kind one wouldn't have been saved.

SAILOR *shakes his head and exits.*

BOOKISH MAN: If you hadn't offered the reward, the sailor would have never jumped into the water …

The End

The Middle Way

Based on the poetry of Attar

Cast

STORYTELLER	Very old, accustomed to hardships in life, knows how to be invisible unless she is telling a story, then she really shines and makes the story come alive.
HANNA	Fatimah's maid, in her 20s, lively, animated, loves a good party, whiny.
GOVERNOR SIKANDER	In her 50s, charismatic, magnanimous, used to getting her own way, suspicious, loving and caring toward her daughter, commanding presence.
PAGE	Quick and attentive.
JAHAN BEGUM	The Governor's daughter, early 20s, very intelligent and beautiful, chooses words carefully, direct.
BEWAFA, a suitor	His name means "insincere" in Urdu, pronounced "Be-waa-feh," accent on the middle syllable. He is arrogant and far too confident, until things don't go his way, and then he is very cowardly. Very flowery, over-done manners.
MAJNOO, a suitor	"Maaj-new," accent on the first syllable, means obsessive love in

	Urdu. He has some mental disorders, plus very bad breath, and he insists on getting in everyone's face, so they all have to deal with his body odor. No manners, far too familiar with total strangers.
SAMID, a suitor	"Sam-id," accent on the first syllable, means "steadfast" in Arabic. He is handsome, thoughtful, doesn't panic easily, and has good manners.
JUDGE	Conservative, uptight, wants all documents to be very organized.
MUFTI	Unconventional, doesn't mind the papers being in complete chaos, so she and judge tussle over how to arrange the papers on the desk.
THREE GUARDS	

Production Notes:

Scene: Governor's Stateroom with large pillars. There are two big chairs (for GOVERNOR and JAHAN BEGUM), a small desk with two chairs, a window on far stage right, and two doors.

STORYTELLER *and* HANNA *are standing*.

HANNA: I never thought I would see Governor Sikander go to such extremes!

STORYTELLER: This can't surprise you that much. All of the Governor's friends pass through here, and at some point they all find an excuse to talk about marriage. They seize the opportunity to mention some young man who, in the friend's opinion, is worthy, properly qualified, and wants nothing less than the Governor's daughter as his bride. "He'll be loving! True!" And so on.

HANNA: Yes, they go on about the young man's qualities, but they are too afraid to formally propose marriage. They make these tactless hints when they ought to speak directly. Why are they all so cowardly?

STORYTELLER: They are afraid their bridegroom candidate will be rejected by the Governor.

HANNA: They are afraid the Governor will give him the thumbs down? Then why put up the young man at all!

STORYTELLER: They are only looking out for themselves. They assume that rejection might sour their friendship between themselves and the Governor.

HANNA: This is an impossible situation.

STORYTELLER: Our Governor is a sharp one; she knows all this. That's why she never allowed the matter to be discussed further. Our Jahan Begum said she would agree to marry someone only if he wants her for herself and not because she is the daughter of the Governor.

HANNA: The fact of the matter is that she is the daughter of the Governor, and that is not going to change, unless there is a regime change.

STORYTELLER: Or an election.

HANNA: Whatever you say, old woman, but this ridiculous announcement at the Autumn Feast, you must admit it is something of a shock.

STORYTELLER: The Governor always says everything has a proper time. She just decided the feast was the proper time.

HANNA: Proper time? Humph. *(Imitating Governor.)* "Today my daughter and I wish to discuss the matter seriously. We must choose one from among the suitors, and we haven't the patience to discuss this at length. Tomorrow my daughter shall marry whomever loves her the most. Therefore, whosoever wishes to press his suit for her hand must come tomorrow morning so that I may tell him the conditions of marriage and for my daughter to see her prospective husband. We can sign the marriage contract and celebrate the wedding on the same day — that is, tomorrow."

STORYTELLER: *(Laughing.)* That is exactly what she said.

HANNA: Well really, do you think this is the proper way to have a wedding? It is too much rushing around. You have to take time to savor these moments. What about all the engagement parties, exchange of gifts, prayers, and hymns for the betrothed?

STORYTELLER: The Governor doesn't like all that; she considers it wasteful.

HANNA: Wasteful! Where is her respect for tradition? Well, you see the result. *(Goes to window and looks out.)* Only three men have shown up.

STORYTELLER: Only three? Oh dear. People must be worried about what the Governor is planning.

HANNA: Have you ever seen a marriage arranged in such a fashion? It's as though this is some kind of contest! And now our dear girl only has three suitors to choose from.

STORYTELLER: All those professed lovers are afraid the Governor might punish them for something. Their fear makes them forget their love.

HANNA: You must admit that in this kind of arrangement there is a possibility of getting into real trouble.

Horns sound; enter PAGE, GOVERNOR, *and* GUARDS.

PAGE: Make way for the Honorable Governor!

GOVERNOR *sits in her chair.* GUARDS *and* PAGE *take up their positions in the Stateroom.*

GOVERNOR: Summon the suitors for my daughter's hand!

One GUARD *exits and re-enters with* BEWAFA, MAJNOO, *and* SAMID. *They stand before the* GOVERNOR.

GOVERNOR: You men are all here today for the hand of my daughter? *(They all nod.)* Very well, please introduce yourselves.

BEWAFA: I am Bewafa, ibn Qushamadi ibn Beyparwah ibn Boozdilli ibn Hassad ibn Shaykh Mutakbar. *(Bows deeply.)*

GOVERNOR: Those names sound familiar, but I haven't met any of those people personally.

BEWAFA: A pity, your Excellency. My lineage is very renown.

GOVERNOR: I see, and you are …

MAJNOO: I am Majnoo. *(Waves.)*

GOVERNOR: Majnoo? *(*MAJNOO *waves.)* Very well. And you there, number three, who are you?

SAMID: I am Samid. *(Small bow.)* I'm studying at the university.

GOVERNOR: So you want to be a scholar. Hrumph. That's enough introductions. Page, go summon my daughter.

PAGE *exits offstage and returns with* JAHAN BEGUM. JAHAN BEGUM *sits next to* GOVERNOR.

GOVERNOR: It is clear that among all the suitors for my daughter's hand, you three are more loving and true. Here is my daughter so that you may see her. If she agrees, we will complete the marriage ceremonies today. *(*GOVERNOR *looks at* JAHAN BEGUM, *who nods her head in acceptance.)* Very well. However, since I am the governor of this city, marriage with my daughter has certain conditions. *(She stands up.)* I shall give you 10 minutes to write your opinion of these conditions on a sheet of paper. Afterward, my daughter and I shall decide in the way we think best and act accordingly. *(*PAGE *starts to distribute paper and quills to suitors.* GOVERNOR *looks to* JAHAN BEGUM, *and she nods modestly.)* The conditions are these: That I tie my daughter's suitor to this pillar *(pats pillar)* and beat him as much as I please. If he is still alive after that, he must live with my daughter wherever we say. They must live on his earnings, however small or great they may be. He must never enter my palace. He must never complain to me about anyone. He must never come to me for a favor. He must not hope for anything from me. If he behaves badly with my daughter and leaves her, I shall order that he be skinned alive! Furthermore, if any of you three, after coming here, does not agree to these conditions, he must leave the city within 48 hours and never return to it. He must never mention me nor my daughter again. If he disobeys these commands, I shall know how to deal with him. *(*GOVERNOR *looks sternly at each suitor.)* You have your paper; now write your replies and sign them. In this way, I shall know to whom I may give my daughter as wife.

GOVERNOR *turns around and sits back in her chair;* GUARDS *escort each suitor to a separate chamber and close the doors and stand guard beside them.*

HANNA: *(To* STORYTELLER.) What did I tell you? Real trouble!

GOVERNOR: Storyteller, come and tell us a tale while we wait for these gentlemen to complete their replies.

STORYTELLER: Very well, your Excellency. One day a holy man was traveling with some companions when they suddenly found the body of a dead dog by the side of the road. The holy man stood looking at the dead dog, and then he said to his companions: "What do you think about this?" They looked at each other, not understanding what he meant. Finally, one answered, "It's the corpse of a dog that has died."

"What an unpleasant smell!" exclaimed one,

"It's a very disturbing sight!" said another.

"How dirty it is!" observed another of the companions.

"Don't touch it!" warned another man. "You might catch some sickness from it."

"When it was alive, being a dog, its body was unclean," said another. "And now that is it dead, it's double unclean!"

"Look!" said another of the companions. "Its mouth is still open. It's as though it wants to bite someone's leg!"

Then the holy man spoke to them: "Everything you have said is true. But you have forgotten something. When this dog was alive, it was a faithful animal. It guarded well and could tell the difference between a friend and a foe. And notice how its teeth are so beautiful and dazzling white!"

So you see, most esteemed personages of this room, in any situation you are in, don't always look at the ugliness and unpleasantness. Whatever you encounter, you should look for goodness and beauty.

Everyone claps and nods with approval at the story.

GOVERNOR: Well done, Storyteller! I really enjoyed that. *(Winks at* JAHAN BEGUM.*)* Perhaps we should check the suitors' teeth! *(They both laugh.* GOVERNOR *turns to* PAGE.*)* Are the judge and the mufti here? Go fetch them now.

Exit PAGE*; re-enter* PAGE *with* JUDGE *and* MUFTI *carrying marriage contracts. They set up at a desk with two chairs and spread out the papers.*

GOVERNOR: Time is up! Bring me the replies! *(*GUARDS *open doors and bring out suitors.* BEWAFA *presents letter to* GOVERNOR, *and she takes it.)* This is one! Bewafa. *(*GOVERNOR *hands paper to* JUDGE. JUDGE *looks it over, stamps it, hands it to* MUFTI. MUFTI *stamps it and hands it back to suitor.* MAJNOO *hands his letter to the* GOVERNOR.*)* Two!

Majnoo. (*Hands letter to* JUDGE *and repeat same as* BEWAFA. SAMID *hands his letter to* GOVERNOR.) Three! Samid. (GOVERNOR *hands letter to* JUDGE *and repeat process*). Now we shall examine them in order.

BEWAFA: *(Reading from his letter.)* Though it is very difficult for me to forget my love, in accordance with the command of Your Excellency, I shall try to leave the city within 48 hours. I pray that Your Excellency not trouble any of my family or relatives; only I was a suitor from among them. No one else has any responsibilities for my actions.

GOVERNOR *and* JAHAN BEGUM *exchange glances and smile.*

GOVERNOR: Very well, the matter of the first suitor is settled. He is not a lover; rather, he is insincere. He wanted my daughter in order to be near me, and he did not want to suffer any trouble for her hand. He does not know that a lover must endure many trials, just as a lover of knowledge and learning must take pains and work hard to become learned. A person who is not steadfast will abandon the difficult path halfway along and flee. This young man is cowardly and thoughtless, too, for he did not imagine that the problem had any other solution. He did not consider that perhaps our conditions were merely a kind of test, or that we might be lenient with him. In any event, each person knows himself best. Therefore, we have nothing more to do with this one. He must leave and never look back. He will forget us, and we shall forget him so that he may rest easy.

JUDGE *snatches* BEWAFA'*s letter and keeps it.* BEWAFA *bows and leaves quickly.*

Exit BEWAFA.

GOVERNOR: Now let us hear from you, Suitor Majnoo.

MAJNOO: *(Reading from letter.)* I accept all of the conditions for marriage and am prepared to do what is required. If I live after the beating, I shall achieve my desire. If I do not live, I shall weep for her in the next world. I don't want to live any other way. Death or the governor's daughter!

GOVERNOR: *(Turns to* JAHAN BEGUM.*)* What do you say, my dear?

JAHAN BEGUM: I don't want a crazy husband!

GOVERNOR: Bravo, my girl! You have spoken well. This one is ready to be tied to a pillar, beaten, and afterwards live at our command like a slave and remain far from me. He is willing to endure hunger and to fear me as though a sword were dangling over his head as long as he lives. *(Looks* MAJNOO *in the eye.)* How is my daughter different from other girls? Why would you buy this love at such a miserable price? *(*GOVERNOR *turns to the others.)* I cannot be confident that this one is sane and in his right mind. He should go to a mental hospital and be treated there. Furthermore, there was nothing about my daughter in his letter. It was all about himself. He is not a true lover; rather he is mad. A mad son-in-law will not do! *(Shaking her head at* MAJNOO.*)* Go quickly and forget us so that we may forget you and that you may be at peace.

JUDGE *gingerly takes* MAJNOO*'s letter and keeps it.* MAJNOO *shrugs shoulders and leaves.*
Exit MAJNOO.

GOVERNOR: Now Suitor Samid, please read your letter.

SAMID: I met the Governor's daughter when my father was in the hospital. Jahan Begum was doing charity work, and every day she would visit him, tell him a story or sing him a song, and listen to his stories and worries. Before he died, he told me that Jahan Begum had all the qualities of an excellent companion: compassion, intelligence, and a good sense of humor. He told me this was the sort of person one wanted as a wife. While I think my father was an excellent judge of character, I have a neighbor who is not bad looking and seems a decent person. But I love the governor's daughter more. I think we shall be happy together. I will not leave the city unless I am forced to do so, and that would be tyranny because I have offended no one. With respect to the other conditions, I also do not like the idea of being beaten and living in fear and apprehension in order to get married. Such a life would not even provide for the happiness of the bride. I am a lover and a suitor only if she too accepts me and the governor reduces the harsh terms of the conditions. If not, well, what is wrong with the neighbor girl next door? I think that for every problem there is a third way to solve it. I pray that the governor will not be offended by my words as I have no quarrel with anyone. Rather, I want to take a wife and live peacefully. Whatever the outcome, I hope for the happiness of the governor's daughter.

GOVERNOR: *(To* JAHAN BEGUM.) What do you say?

JAHAN BEGUM: Whatever you command. No one else has come.

GOVERNOR: *(Laughing.)* Very good! This young man is intelligent. He doubts that there is any real difference between my daughter and the daughter of his neighbor, but since he loves mine more, he thinks you both would live more happily together. This young man is intelligent because he neither fled from fear nor did he accept a beating out of madness. Rather he found a third way, a middle way. Know, young man, that my conditions were a test. I, too, wish for the happiness of my daughter. Now the choice is yours. Are you ready to complete the marriage ceremonies right now and without any special conditions? If you are not, I hope that you will be happy with your neighbor girl, and we shall be present at your wedding to congratulate you. Now what do you say?

SAMID: I came here with great hopes and desires.

JAHAN BEGUM: I, too.

GOVERNOR: And I with the greatest pleasure announce your betrothal. I pray that God may bless you and grant you both a long and happy life together.

STORYTELLER: There is justice in the middle way.

HANNA: Praise be to God. And now I have a wedding to plan!

The End

Notes: Bewafa's name means Insincere, and his lineage is: Insincere, son of Flattery, son of Thoughtlessness, son of Cowardly, son of Envy, son of Shaykh Arrogant.

A Beggar's Remedy

Based on the poetry of Attar

Cast

SCRIBE	Very well-spoken, well-educated, acts arrogant around "the masses," humble around those of higher status than herself.
BEGGAR ALI	Charismatic, lazy, a good storyteller, very charming when he wants to be, manipulative.
PEDDLER	Hardworking, honest, simple.
GUARD	Bored and sleepy.
GATE GUARD	Alert and suspicious.
BAKER	Good-tempered but doesn't tolerate nonsense.
FOOD KITCHEN WORKER	Airport security guard mentality.
FIRST CITIZEN OF NISHAPUR	In a hurry.
SECOND CITIZEN OF NISHAPUR	Sarcastic and insensitive.
TWO SCHOOLGIRLS	Energetic and giggle easily.
UNDERCOVER BEGGAR	At first she looks really pathetic, weak, poor, and potentially "under the influence," but actually quite competent and observant.

BACKSTREET MAN	Conservative, cares about appearances, likes to brag about his town.
GOVERNOR OF NISHAPUR	Magnanimous, a bit insensitive, a good listener, but hard to capture her attention for long periods of time.
MASTER HUNTSMAN	"Outdoorsy," a man's man, the strong, silent type.
HOSPITAL WORKER	Doesn't trust people, forceful, competent at job.
WORKHOUSE FOREMAN	30s, very busy to the point of getting easily distracted, wants to help everyone.
WASHERWOMAN	Very old, weak, moves slowly, knows the history of the city.
BLACKSMITH	Loud, physical, jovial.
SMALL BOY	Quick, lively, a good listener.
CITIZEN OF SABZEVAR	Nouveau-riche, acts without thinking.

Production Notes:

The scene where the beggar and peddler are standing "outside the city gates" could be simply played in front of the curtain. When the gates are "opened," just open the curtain to reveal the town.

Cast Substitutions: First Guard = Master Huntsman, Peddler = Blacksmith, Baker = Citizen of Sabzevar, one of the Schoolgirls= Small boy, First Citizen of Nishapur =

Washerwoman, Second Citizen of Nishapur = Hospital Worker, one of the Schoolgirls = Workhouse Foreman.

The last scene in the town of Sabzevar can also be played in front of closed curtains. Make a fabric curtain backdrop for a blacksmith's shop and just a few props to indicate a working smithy.

Scene 1. Stage is dark; spotlight on one place.

Enter SCRIBE.

SCRIBE: Shaykh Farid ad-Din Abu Hamid Muhammad was born in Kadkan, a town near Nishapur in the province of Khorasan, now in modern Iran, at the time of the Seljuk Empire. He was born around 1136 Common Era and by all accounts lived a very long life. Some believe he lived into his 90s. His father was a perfume maker, and the word for perfumer is "Attar" in both Persian and Arabic. Attar was the pen name that Farid ad-Din chose for himself when he started writing poetry. In Attar's time, perfumers were often doctors and pharmacists who mixed herbs and medicines together to help people. Attar was said to be a skilled pharmacist, as well as a maker of perfume.

    It is said that after his pilgrimage to Mecca, Attar devoted himself to Sufism. His main concern was with direct communication and eventual unity of the soul with God.

    Attar wrote many important books. His most famous works were *Mantiq-at-Ta'ir*, or *The Conference of the Birds*, *Musibat-namah*, or *The Book of Hardship*, and *Ilahi-namah*, or *The Divine Book*. The story you are about to see is drawn from this last volume.

    Please join us as we travel back eight centuries to the world of Attar and medieval Persia. We hope you enjoy the story of "A Beggar's Remedy."

Scene 2. Early morning, just after sunrise, at the walled city of Nishapur in front of the city gates.

GUARD *stands at attention.*

Enter PEDDLER *from stage left. She stands against wall waiting.*

Enter BEGGAR ALI *stage right; crosses guard and gate and goes over to* PEDDLER.

BEGGAR ALI: Peace be upon you.

PEDDLER: And on you.

BEGGAR ALI: Is this indeed the gate to the city of Nishapur?

PEDDLER: Yes, it certainly is. What business brings you to the city?

BEGGAR ALI: I am here to ply my trade.

PEDDLER: And what might that be?

BEGGAR ALI: I, madam, am a beggar.

PEDDLER: Oh, my brother. You have made a big mistake. Haven't you heard about the city of Nishapur?

BEGGAR ALI: I have heard that it is an important and prosperous city.

PEDDLER: This much is true; however, they have a law that directly affects you.

BEGGAR ALI: What's that?

PEDDLER: No one is allowed to beg within the city.

BEGGAR ALI: Not allowed to beg? Preposterous! I've never heard of such a rule, much less it being enforced with any success.

PEDDLER: Things are different here. You'll see. You'd best not tell anyone you're a beggar if you wish to enter the city.

BEGGAR ALI: Well thank you for the advice, friend.

PEDDLER: Have you always been a beggar?

BEGGAR ALI: Actually, no. When I was 10 years old, I was apprenticed to a blacksmith. I worked hard, and I received 10 coppers a day.

PEDDLER: That's not very much money.

BEGGAR ALI: No, it wasn't.

PEDDLER: Is that why you quit the apprenticeship?

BEGGAR ALI: It's a bit more complicated. You see, one day I was sent with a jug to fetch some water from the well. On the way, I dropped the jug and broke it. I was afraid that if I returned to the shop empty-handed, the blacksmith would scold me — or worse.

PEDDLER: Yes, an angry blacksmith is not a good thing!

BEGGAR ALI: So, I sat down in that very spot, and I started to cry. The next thing I knew, an old man pressed a copper coin into my hand and said, "Don't cry lad." "But sir," I protested, "I'm not a beggar; the jug belonged to my boss." The old man replied, "That's all right. Take the coin and buy a new jug. The blacksmith won't scold you. A new jug will cost just one copper."

PEDDLER: I don't understand; it sounds like your problem was solved by the old man's generosity.

BEGGAR ALI: Well, it's complicated. The old man went on his way, and I just sat there staring at the broken jug and the coin. Then, a woman came along and she gave me a coin! She told me to stop crying and buy a new jug.

PEDDLER: I think I see the problem here.

BEGGAR ALI: Just so! Now I had enough for two jugs. I was so amazed at this prospect, that as I was sitting there …

PEDDLER: Someone else gave you a copper coin.

BEGGAR ALI: Exactly, my sister! As more people passed by me, many of them gave me small coins. My eyes were opened. I worked in that blacksmith's shop from dawn to dusk, and all I ever earned was 10 lousy copper coins. But by sitting for half an hour with that broken jug, I earned 20, and I didn't have to endure the blacksmith's rough words and abuse!

PEDDLER: That broken jug created a very unusual incentive for you.

BEGGAR ALI: I'll never forget the look on my master's face when I left him.

PEDDLER: You faced him again?

BEGGAR ALI: Well you see, when it was noon, a woman came out of her house and brought me a jug similar to the one that lay in pieces in front of me. She gave it to me and told me to fill it with water and finish my errand. I told her I was late and my boss would beat me. She went with me to the smithy and told him that the broken jug was not my fault, there was a big line at the well, and not to blame me as I would be more careful next time.

PEDDLER: But surely, the blacksmith took you back in.

BEGGAR ALI: Not exactly. He was polite to the woman, but after she left, he told me that after I broke the jug I should have hurried back and told him instead of saying bad things about him to the townsfolk.

PEDDLER: So he thought you were a gossip?

BEGGAR ALI: He said as much. He said, "I don't want an apprentice who brings dishonor on me. Take the 10 coppers for today's work and be off with you! If you weren't a beggar by nature, you wouldn't have taken money and things from people."

PEDDLER: He thought you were a beggar by nature? Curious.

BEGGAR ALI: I didn't know what to say to him. I just took the money and left.

Peddler: What did you do next?

BEGGAR ALI: I didn't want the street in front of the kind woman to be messy, so I thought I would go clean up the pieces of the broken jug. I collected the pieces, but I thought that if I went home too early, my stepmother would quarrel with me. To avoid a big fight, I went to a different street, laid the pieces of the jug at the foot of a wall and sat next to them.

PEDDLER: With tears streaming down your face?

BEGGAR ALI: Before the waterworks started, I thought I should look for an omen regarding my new profession. I drew lines in the dirt, called one "good" and one "bad," and made my calculations.

PEDDLER: Your dirt line omens told you it would be favorable to take up begging.

BEGGAR ALI: Actually, no. The omen was bad. But, I decided to stay and see what would happen.

PEDDLER: And what exactly happened?

BEGGAR ALI: People would come along, see my broken jug, and ask me about it. I'd tell them I broke my boss' jug, and they'd give me some money.

PEDDLER: Are you trying to tell me that the generosity of the villagers drove you into becoming a beggar?

BEGGAR ALI: No my sister, it is not that simple. Although I did not understand it that day, over my years of begging I have come to realize this simple truth. The people who shower coins on me seek to gain a reward from God for themselves. They didn't care about me; they didn't care if I learned anything. They were just interested in a blessing for themselves.

PEDDLER: Well, it has been my experience that a person will employ her brains to advance whatever line of work she chooses, or in your case, into which he falls. One person works in industry and makes new things. And you, my friend, will have to improve your skills in begging if you want to make it in this city of Nishapur.

BEGGAR ALI: Oh my friend, I have perfected my art. I am a Master Beggar. I am very capable of making myself look more miserable and poorer than I actually am.

PEDDLER: I can't say I'm surprised.

BEGGAR ALI: Once I pretended my hand was paralyzed. Another time I dragged my foot as though I were lame. I always rub dirt in my clothes. Once I pretended to faint; that was quite effective. With all my strategies, people gave me more and more money. What need do I have to work? Besides, people like it this way, in every town I have visited. They just want a blessing.

PEDDLER: Nishapur is different. You will see.

BEGGAR ALI: Yes, I shall.

Bell clangs loudly three times. GUARD *stands at attention. Doors to city slowly open. A new* GATE GUARD *comes out and takes the place of the old* GUARD. *The* PEDDLER *and* BEGGAR *get in line.*

GATE GUARD: *(To* PEDDLER.*)* Who are you? What is your business?

PEDDLER: I am a peddler. I sell needles, thread, scissors, and I sharpen knives.

GATE GUARD: Where do you come from?

PEDDLER: Ghazni.

GATE GUARD: Very well, come inside and go about your business.

Exit PEDDLER *through city gates.*

GATE GUARD: *(Looking at Beggar Ali.)* Who are you? What is your business? Where do you come from, and do you have any money?

BEGGAR ALI: I come from Abarqu on the other side of the great desert. I am poor and miserable, but I have a little money.

GATE GUARD: Do you know any trade?

BEGGAR ALI: Of course. I am a blacksmith.

GATE GUARD: A blacksmith? Where are your tools?

BEGGAR ALI: Lost in a sandstorm. I'm hoping my luck will change in your fair city.

GATE GUARD: Sand storm, eh? Hmm. You may enter, but mind that you don't beg in Nishapur! The citizens don't want beggars here, and they don't give money to them.

BEGGAR ALI: Certainly.

GATE GUARD: You may enter.

Exit BEGGAR ALI *through city gates.*

Scene 3. Inside the city of Nishapur, with a Bakery, Public Kitchen, other shops, and walled tomb of Shaykh Attar.

BEGGAR ALI *spots the bakery and goes over to the door.* BAKER *stands in the door.* BEGGAR ALI *extends his hands in begging gesture.*

BEGGAR ALI: *(Whining.)* May God extend your life. In God's way, give this poor person some bread.

BAKER: May God lengthen your life, too. My prayer is your prayer, but it is obvious that you are a stranger here and you do not know that begging is illegal in Nishapur.

BEGGAR ALI: Illegal? Illegal! If someone is hungry, then what is he to do?

BAKER: If someone is hungry, he should go to the local public kitchen. They'll give him something to eat.

BEGGAR ALI: Give him some ...? Where is this public kitchen?

BAKER: Just keep walking that way. *(Points finger.)*

BEGGAR ALI *walks to public kitchen. He goes up to the* FOOD KITCHEN WORKER.

BEGGAR ALI: I'm a stranger here. I don't have anything to eat.

FOOD KITCHEN WORKER: *(Starts to pat* BEGGAR ALI *down, then goes through his pockets.)* You say you don't have anything to eat, but you have money. *(Holds up* BEGGAR ALI*'s money;* BEGGAR ALI *snatches it away and puts it back in his pocket.)* Use your money to buy food and then go to the workhouse, and they'll give you work to do. No one in this city gives anyone bread for free. This public kitchen is for people who don't have a single coin.

BEGGAR ALI: Suppose someone is sick and cannot work.

FOOD KITCHEN WORKER: Then he must go to the local hospital and be treated. If he can't be treated successfully, then they will send him to the local jail.

BEGGAR ALI: Well, thank you for that information.

FOOD KITCHEN WORKER: Peace be upon you.

BEGGAR ALI: And on you.

BEGGAR ALI *walks away. When he thinks he is out of the* FOOD KITCHEN WORKER*'s hearing, he talks to himself.*

BEGGAR ALI: This is utter nonsense. I'll go and beg as usual.

Enter FIRST CITIZEN OF NISHAPUR. BEGGAR ALI *sees the woman; he approaches her, hands outstretched.*

BEGGAR ALI: May God grant you health!

FIRST CITIZEN OF NISHAPUR: If you know any prayers, then pray for yourself. We also know prayers: May God give you life! May God help you! God have mercy on your father and mother!

BEGGAR ALI *looks at her in surprise and shrugs his shoulders.*

Exit FIRST CITIZEN OF NISHAPUR.

Enter SECOND CITIZEN OF NISHAPUR. BEGGAR ALI *approaches him, hands outstretched.*

BEGGAR ALI: It's Friday Eve, and the eve of the first of the month!

SECOND CITIZEN OF NISHAPUR: The eve of the first of the month to the eve of the last of the month! It's all the same. Night is night. Friday Eve is not yours to sell; it belongs to everyone. Friday is for those who work six days a week.

BEGGAR ALI: Curse you for your miserliness!

SECOND CITIZEN OF NISHAPUR: We know curses, too, but they are a kind of nuisance. Creating a nuisance can get you a fine here.

Exit SECOND CITIZEN OF NISHAPUR.

Enter TWO SCHOOLGIRLS, *carrying baskets of food.*

BEGGAR ALI: Please ladies, can you not spare some food? I am so hungry.

GIRL 1: If you are hungry, go get a hot meal from the public kitchen.

GIRL 2: The public kitchen is just there, past the bakery.

Exit TWO SCHOOLGIRLS.

Enter UNDERCOVER BEGGAR.

BEGGAR ALI: Sister! How do you survive in this city? I can't get anything out of these people.

UNDERCOVER BEGGAR: The people of this place are charitable to those who work. If someone gives alms to someone for no purpose, he'll be fined by the governor. Begging is illegal here, and so is giving to beggars or encouraging them.

BEGGAR ALI: But then, why are you a beggar?

UNDERCOVER BEGGAR: I'm not a beggar. I'm an employee of the Public Inspectorate. My job is to dress up like a beggar and roam about to see if anyone will break the law and give me money. If someone does, I arrest her and take her to the court to fine her for encouraging begging and beggars!

BEGGAR ALI: This is the most absurd, nonsensical city I have ever had the misfortune to visit. What do the people do when they want to give charity or alms? Are mercy and generosity now become sins?

UNDERCOVER BEGGAR: No, mercy and generosity are very good, but here everyone who wishes to give alms and charity puts his money in the box for the needy. The money is collected and spent for those who must eat at the public kitchen or are in the poorhouse and are infirm or feeble. An able-bodied person must work. There is a workhouse in every quarter, and work to be done is given those who are out of work.

BEGGAR ALI: Thank you very much. It's plain that because of these arrangements, there is nothing to do except work. Begging won't bring any free bread.

UNDERCOVER BEGGAR: No, it won't. Peace be upon you.

BEGGAR ALI: And on you.

Exit UNDERCOVER BEGGAR.

BEGGAR ALI *sees an old bucket and picks it up.*

BEGGAR ALI: I'll carry this bucket with me, and no one will know that I am a beggar. I'll pretend I'm a pool cleaner! Then I can beg in some of the quieter streets where there aren't so many spies to see me. If someone tries to get me to empty his garden pool, I'll say that my foot hurts and pretend that I'm not able. In the end, people will feel sorry for me. The women are better than the men in that respect. Everything will be all right as soon as I start crying, "Ladies! Ladies! For the health of your children! I haven't eaten anything today!"

BEGGAR ALI *takes the bucket and goes out into the audience.*

BEGGAR ALI: Pool water! Pool water! I change pool water! I beat rugs, too! Pool water!*(Go down another aisle.)* Ladies! Ladies! *(In audience,* BACKSTREET MAN *stands up.)*

BACKSTREET MAN: What is going on here? Why are you disturbing the people's peace? What is this shouting? Don't you know that shouting in a public place is illegal? If the inspector sees you, you'll be taken to court. (BACKSTREET MAN *walks slowly with* BEGGAR ALI *toward the main stage.*)

BEGGAR ALI: To court? For what?

BACKSTREET MAN: For creating a kind of public nuisance. Now, I'm a decent fellow, and I don't like to bother anyone, but be careful and watch your step.

BEGGAR ALI: (*Shrugs his shoulders and starts shouting.*) Pool water!

BACKSTREET MAN: Don't shout in the street! People are trying to rest in their homes!

BEGGAR ALI: My good fellow! Since you are a good man, tell me what I should do. I'm a stranger here and don't know what I should do in this city. Is cleaning garden pools something bad? Is one permitted to sell soapwort?

BACKSTREET MAN: Yes, a person can buy and sell anything freely that is not harmful to people. However, you can't shout and hawk wares loudly in the streets of Nishapur. It is illegal. Noise pollution.

BEGGAR ALI: Noise pollution?

BACKSTREET MAN: Yes. If you want to sell soapwort, you must find a spot and then sell it quietly. Just as people have ears, they have eyes. If someone needs some soapwort, he'll come to you where you are and buy it from you. If he doesn't want any, well, he won't be bothered by the shouting.

BEGGAR ALI: As you say, sir. But tell me one thing: Who takes care of the garden pools in this city?

BACKSTREET MAN: The public works office. They send laborers to do it. They also have a division that collects trash. There are shops to handle cleaning rugs. There are stores to buy clothing and other things. There's no need to go about the streets shouting. That's old-fashioned.

BEGGAR ALI: But what to you do about old, dry bread? Do you throw it into the trash?

BACKSTREET MAN: No sir! We don't throw it into the trash. Everything is well-organized here. The dry bread is collected, and once a week men from the local poultry farm collective come and buy it. The money they pay is used for the needy. There is a box for money to be used by the needy in every street and lane. We don't return old bread to the baker so that he can mix it with the fresh bread.

BEGGAR ALI: Excellent. But what can a person like me do? I'm a stranger here, and I don't have any food. I don't have money to pay for a room in an inn.

BACKSTREET MAN: *(Laughs.)* The first day you eat at the public kitchen. The first night you can sleep in the public dormitory. The next day go work and be paid. We have plenty of jobs here. In short, there is no place for begging in this city. The reason is that the people do not want to turn others into beggars.

BEGGAR ALI: I understand. Peace be upon you, brother.

BACKSTREET MAN: And on you

Exit BACKSTREET MAN.

BEGGAR ALI: *(Walking back to main stage.)* They've thought of everything. Public kitchen, poultry farm, jail, poorhouse, undercover beggars, workhouse, public dormitory, jobs … When people don't want to make more beggars and don't encourage begging then everything is fine. Make jobs, not alms! I wasn't always a beggar. Once I was a blacksmith's apprentice, and my name was Master Ali. I wasn't Beggar Ali. People made me a beggar thinking only of their own spiritual reward. God punish them for that! Where is there justice in this? *(*BEGGAR ALI *sees the* GOVERNOR, SCRIBE, *and* MASTER HUNTSMAN *entering.)*

Enter GOVERNOR OF NISHAPUR, SCRIBE, *and* MASTER HUNTSMAN.

BEGGAR ALI: What kind of city is this in which I can be so unfortunate? They claim their Governor is just? This is not justice, this is …

GOVERNOR OF NISHAPUR: What are you doing?

BEGGAR ALI: Nothing.

GOVERNOR OF NISHAPUR: I just heard you talking and complaining. Who has done an injustice to you?

BEGGAR ALI: I don't know. There wasn't anyone here to complain to, but my life is very hard.

GOVERNOR OF NISHAPUR: I heard you mention the Governor. Do you have any complaint about her?

BEGGAR ALI: Are you the Governor?

GOVERNOR OF NISHAPUR: Yes, I am. People consider me just.

BEGGAR ALI: In my opinion, whoever calls you just should have his mouth stuffed with dirt because he is lying. Is it any justice that I beg for 30 long years around this country and get no reward from life? My stomach is empty, yet you are the governor, and you are called just.

GOVERNOR OF NISHAPUR: It is true that you appear to be very unfortunate. I didn't know anything about your plight until just now. Can you forget the past and let me send you to a hospital to be treated?

BEGGAR ALI: I am not sick. I don't need to go to the hospital. My problem is misfortune and poverty.

GOVERNOR OF NISHAPUR: Very well, I am pleased that you speak the truth so plainly. Bad fortune is not cured with medicine; it is cured with good fortune. That is something that all people search for. Everyone wants to find opportunities to improve their lives. If people do not strive to improve their lives, there won't be anything left in the world, and the world will become a desert. But, tell me, what have you been doing in your search for a better life?

BEGGAR ALI: What have I been doing? I've traveled all over this land for 30 years. Wherever I knocked on a door, it has been shut on me. What can I do? The rest should be asked of you who are the just Governor of Nishapur.

GOVERNOR OF NISHAPUR: All right, if I am asked I shall answer that you have a right to prosper. Of course, all people are not the same. Everyone cannot be very learned, rich, and powerful. Yet everyone has a right to her portion in life and to peace, and so do you. Now I shall order that we learn who has your portion. They will give you what they owe you.

BEGGAR ALI: But no one owes me anything. What I'm saying is that if you are just, I should get my just dues.

GOVERNOR OF NISHAPUR: So, if no one owes you anything, do you know who has stolen that which is your right? Have I taken it?

BEGGAR ALI: No, you haven't taken anything from me, but there is so much affluence and comfort in life all around me. Where is mine?

GOVERNOR OF NISHAPUR: Prosperity is everywhere. But it is like this: If you are thirsty, don't you have to extend your arm and take the water jug and drink from it? Life is like that. If you want to make your life better, you have to get busy yourself and go after it.

BEGGAR ALI: If I reach out, they'll call me a thief! Or they'll say that I'm a beggar, and they won't let me get anything.

GOVERNOR OF NISHAPUR: I'm not suggesting that you try to take or beg things from others. What I mean is that just as you must make an effort to lift the water jug in order to get your drink of water, so you must make your own efforts to improve your life. You have to agree that 30 years of wandering and begging has not made you rich nor happy. You have to try another way to save yourself from poverty and all this complaining about your life.

BEGGAR ALI: That's right. I should do something else, but I don't have any other skill.

GOVERNOR OF NISHAPUR: Tell me, have I taken away your job from you?

BEGGAR ALI: No, I didn't have a job for you to take. I don't know what to say.

GOVERNOR OF NISHAPUR: I know what you want to say. You want good clothes. You want good food. You want a good home. You want a wife, children, honor, and respect. If you cannot be, for example, a royal minister, you want to be like other people who have quiet, prosperous lives.

BEGGAR ALI: Yes, that's it. That's what I want. If I had such things, I wouldn't have any complaints about the governor!

GOVERNOR OF NISHAPUR: Well then, everyone must work or no one will have anything, and I would not have a city to govern.

BEGGAR ALI: Who will give me a job?

GOVERNOR OF NISHAPUR: A good question. Now that I know you, I shall give you a job, a good job, an honorable job, but only if you yourself want it. Are you prepared to come tomorrow and take the place of my scribe and do what she does? You will have her responsibilities, her power, and her respect. (SCRIBE *looks very unhappy.)*

BEGGAR ALI: No, I do not possess the knowledge and wisdom of your scribe. I can't do her job. As soon as they find out that I don't have her skill, you will criticize me and others will also, and my life will be disgraced.

GOVERNOR OF NISHAPUR: All right, if you can't or don't want to take the place of my scribe, would you like to come with me today and take the place of the chief huntsman? You would organize the hunt, and I'll appoint him to some other position. You will receive his salary and all the privileges that go with the job. (MASTER HUNTSMAN *looks very unhappy)*

BEGGAR ALI: No, what do I know about leading a hunt? I know nothing about organizing a hunt. If I were to take the job, no one would obey me, and everything would fall apart.

GOVERNOR OF NISHAPUR: So that's not suitable for you either? Look, I'm ready to give you a job at the court, but you won't accept one! Perhaps you would accept a different kind of job. Would you agree to work in my library with the other librarians and scholars?

BEGGAR ALI: No, I can't read and write. What can I do with books?

GOVERNOR OF NISHAPUR: How odd. You mean you have been traveling about this country for 30 years and haven't even learned the alphabet? Dear friend, you could have learned that in three months! If you had spent one hour a week during those years in a library, you could have prepared yourself for some profession better than begging. But, it's not too late. I'm not trying to blame you. You can still earn. I want to wake you up.

BEGGAR ALI: I'm wide awake. I know a hundred illiterates who have millions!

GOVERNOR OF NISHAPUR: That's so, but none of them complain about lack of work. They didn't get their money from my treasury. They worked and earned what they have with effort, brains, and ambition.

BEGGAR ALI: Or they inherited it.

GOVERNOR OF NISHAPUR: An inheritance would be their parents' property. Anyway, if you know hundreds that inherited their money, I know thousands who worked for theirs. All right, now tell me, what is my shortcoming in your affairs?

BEGGAR ALI: You should have done something to make me happy.

GOVERNOR OF NISHAPUR: That's not the way things are. You have already answered your own complaints when you say you know many illiterates who have millions. If the responsibility for your misfortune is mine, then I may say that I have ruled so that a hundred illiterates have made their fortunes. They consider me just. If the responsibility is not mine, then what have I to do with your good or bad fortune? You have already refused the jobs I have offered you, but you haven't told me what you want me to do. Should I order the treasury to give you a thousand pieces of silver?

BEGGAR ALI: That wouldn't be a bad idea!

GOVERNOR OF NISHAPUR: As a matter of fact, it would be a very bad idea. The money in the treasury is not my money; it belongs to the people and the kingdom. If I gave their money to you, the people would no longer say that I am just.

BEGGAR ALI: Yes, they would call you a tyrant. Well then, what should I do?

GOVERNOR OF NISHAPUR: Now that you ask that question, you're coming to your senses. Let's see: What should be done in your case? *(To* SCRIBE *and* MASTER HUNTSMAN.*)* You two: Any suggestions for this man?

SCRIBE: You have come to realize your situation a little late in life.

MASTER HUNTSMAN: You should have been thinking about learning some trade when you were much younger. It doesn't matter what. Any good trade would do for you. If you had learned to be a carpenter, a blacksmith, a tailor, a mason, a farmer, or any of a thousand other trades, you would be a master at it now.

SCRIBE: If you had studied something during these 30 years instead of wandering aimlessly, you might be a scholar now.

MASTER HUNTSMAN: If you had gotten up and done something useful, such as sweeping a street, you would begin to regain your self-respect.

SCRIBE: If you had some self-respect, you would begin to drive away misfortune and open the door of good fortune. But instead, you sit here and complain about the Governor. That won't help anything.

BEGGAR ALI: *(Bowing to* GOVERNOR.*)* I understand now that I have neglected my own duty to myself and the world. This very day I shall go and start to work in something. There are a thousand things I can do. I have been flying from work, but there is something else I want to know. What does the justice of Nishapur mean?

GOVERNOR OF NISHAPUR: For me, it means that I take care that people do not act unjustly to themselves. That the people pay attention to their own affairs and are hopeful for a better future. That they benefit from their own labor and abilities. I made a very good oath to the people when I took office. Scribe? Could you please read my inauguration speech.

SCRIBE: Your Excellency?

GOVERNOR OF NISHAPUR: Now. Go on; read it.

SCRIBE: As you wish. *(Looks through bag of scrolls. Pulls one out.)* Here it is, one of your favorites. *(Reads from scroll.)* "I have been given authority over you, but I am not the best among you. If I do well, help me; and if I do wrong, correct me. We must be loyal to the truth, and disregard for truth is treachery. The weak among you shall be strong in my eyes until I have secured your rights, if God wills it; and the strong among you shall be weak with me until I have wrested from you the rights of others, if God wills it. God have mercy upon us all!"

GOVERNOR OF NISHAPUR: Now that is an acceptance speech!

SCRIBE: Inspiring.

MASTER HUNTSMAN: Well said.

BEGGAR ALI: Now I want to work and study. Since I am in the presence of the Governor of Nishapur, let her do something to make my journey shorter.

GOVERNOR OF NISHAPUR: Master Huntsman, take this unfortunate man to the workhouse foreman to give him some work. If he can be fortunate in life, let him be so! Peace be upon you!

MASTER HUNTSMAN and BEGGAR ALI: And on you, your Excellency.

Exit GOVERNOR OF NISHAPUR *and* SCRIBE.

MASTER HUNTSMAN *and* BEGGAR ALI *start to walk, then* BEGGAR ALI *stumbles.*

MASTER HUNTSMAN: Are you all right?

BEGGAR ALI: My foot, I can't move it.

MASTER HUNTSMAN: Come, let us go to the hospital.

(They walk over to hospital, BEGGAR ALI *leaning on* MASTER HUNTSMAN *and limping)*

BEGGAR ALI: Thank you, thank you friend; you may leave me. I will be in good hands here.

MASTER HUNTSMAN: Very well, peace be upon you.

BEGGAR ALI: And on you.

Exit MASTER HUNTSMAN.

HOSPITAL WORKER: What seems to be the problem?

BEGGAR ALI: I can't move my foot. It is paralyzed.

HOSPITAL WORKER: *(Examines foot.)* Your foot is fine. There is nothing wrong with it.

BEGGAR ALI: Well, now that you mention it, my foot does feel better.

HOSPITAL WORKER: Look, I can't keep you here if you are healthy. If you're poor, then go to the local work office. They'll pay you at the end of the day, and you can buy food.

BEGGAR ALI: I give up. Nishapur is different from other cities, and I feel different, too. Take me to the work office.

BEGGAR ALI *and* HOSPITAL WORKER *walk over to the Work Office and knock. Enter* WORKHOUSE FOREMAN.

BEGGAR ALI: I need some work.

WORKHOUSE FOREMAN: Well, you have come to the right place. Wait here a minute. *(He goes inside shop, returns, and gives* BEGGAR ALI *a sieve and a broom.*) Go to Maliki Street and sweep the street with this broom. Then, separate the sweepings with the sieve. Put the dirt in the barrel and the other trash in the garbage can. When you've finished, come back, and take your money.

Exit HOSPITAL WORKER.

BEGGAR ALI *begins to sweep the street. He sings a song while he works.*

BEGGAR ALI: Sweeping the street, so I can eat. Sweeping the street, so I can eat. Guv'ner say "Workin' makes you a man. Thirty years a beggar ain't no plan. Why can't you learn to read and write? Why don't you go fly a kite?" Sweeping the street, so I can eat. Sweeping the street, so I can. Eat. *(He finishes the job and returns to the* FOREMAN.*)*

WORKHOUSE FOREMAN: Good job sweeping that street. It looks much better. Here are your wages. *(Hands* BEGGAR ALI *some coins.)*

BEGGAR ALI: *(Holding coins.)* This is the first time in many years when I have actually held a coin that I earned by my own efforts. A real job. Not the best job, but my work did make the street look nicer. Maybe it even prevented dust from getting in someone's eyes. Where do I go next?

WORKHOUSE FOREMAN: You need to go wash the stone walls of the Tomb of Shaykh Attar. *(Hands* BEGGAR ALI *a bucket and sponges.)* Over there. *(Points finger to far stage.)*

BEGGAR ALI *goes to walls.* WASHERWOMAN *is also washing the walls.* BEGGAR ALI *starts to wash the walls.*

BEGGAR ALI: Peace be upon you sister.

WASHERWOMAN: And on you.

BEGGAR ALI: So, do you know anything about this saint, whose tomb we are washing?

WASHERWOMAN: He wasn't a saint; it is Shaykh Attar.

BEGGAR ALI: Well, who was this Shaykh Attar?

WASHERWOMAN: Some say he was a dervish; others say he was a recluse. But I will say this: He worked more than anyone else.

BEGGAR ALI: A tomb for a hard worker?

WASHERWOMAN: He was a pharmacist, and he made medicines that made many sick people well.

They start to wash the walls.

BEGGAR ALI: What is this written on the wall?

WASHERWOMAN: They do that; they write poetry on the tomb. Sometimes the poems are the ones Attar wrote; other times they are new, written by the young people.

BEGGAR ALI: Well, what does this one say?

WASHERWOMAN: Hmm, now this one, this was written by Attar himself. It says,
"Strive with your whole being to become as a bird to find God; Strive with your whole being to develop your wings and your feathers."

BEGGAR ALI *has an epiphany. He leans against the wall.*

BEGGAR ALI: *(To audience.)* I swear I will never beg again. I don't want to be called Beggar Ali anymore. I want to become Master Ali again. (*To* WASHERWOMAN.) Thank you for reading this poem for me. There is something important I must do. Peace be upon you.

WASHERWOMAN: And on you.

BEGGAR ALI *goes to the* WORKHOUSE FOREMAN.

BEGGAR ALI: Please sir, I am tired of these small jobs. Long ago I was apprenticed to a blacksmith; I still remember what he taught me. Can I find work with a smithy?

WORKHOUSE FOREMAN: Wonderful! My brother-in-law is a blacksmith who could use an extra pair of hands. Follow me!

Exit BEGGAR ALI *and* WORKHOUSE FOREMAN.

As curtains close, enter SCRIBE *center stage.*

SCRIBE: The beggar is transformed into a respectable blacksmith by a few words from a poet's tomb. Do you believe this? Can you believe this? Do you think poetry can change your life for the better? Let's examine the facts, ladies and gentlemen. Fast forward a year later, and let's see how Ali fares in a different environment, this time the City of Sabzevar.

Scene 4. City of Sabzevar. Blacksmith shop set up.

YOUNG BOY *comes running out with a big jug.* BEGGAR ALI *follows behind him*

BEGGAR ALI: Dear boy, slow down and be careful not to break this jug. But if you do break it, don't get upset about it. A jug is not more important than you. Just come back, and I'll buy another one. And, if you break a jug, don't wait around the broken pieces. Collect them and throw them into the trash and run away from that place as fast as you can! Run away!

YOUNG BOY *nods, walks off more slowly with the big jug.* Enter BLACKSMITH, *coming out of shop.*

BLACKSMITH: Craftsman Ali, you seem very concerned with the quality of jugs.

BEGGAR ALI: I know something that makes me dislike breaking water jugs.

BLACKSMITH: What do you think of this city of Sabzevar?

BEGGAR ALI: It is all right, I suppose. How long are we visiting?

BLACKSMITH: That depends on how fast we work. The horseshoes of Nishapur have gotten to be quite famous in our region. A lot of this is thanks to your skill.

BEGGAR ALI: A well-made horseshoe is a beautiful thing.

BLACKSMITH: Your famous horseshoes have pleased the Governor of Nishapur. As a gesture of good will, our Governor has put us on loan to the Governor of Sabzevar. Once we have shoes on all the governor of Sabzevar's horses, we can be on our way. I'm going to stoke the forge now so we can start the day.

Exit BLACKSMITH.

BEGGAR ALI *moves to the front of the shop. Enter* CITIZEN OF SABZEVAR. *He sees* BEGGAR ALI *and gives him a coin.*

BEGGAR ALI: *(Shocked.)* What is this?

CITIZEN OF SABZEVAR: Money. Aren't you poor?

BEGGAR ALI: You're the poor man! It's been a while since I was poor. I'm an honest workman. I have a job, and I live with honor and respect. Do you want me to become a beggar again? It's too bad that you aren't in Nishapur so that I could take you to court and have you fined!

CITIZEN OF SABZEVAR: *(Shocked.)* Fined? Why?

BEGGAR ALI: Because the people of Nishapur don't want to make other people into beggars. And the Governor of that city knows how to cure them of the habit!

The End

The Packsaddle Maker's School

Based on poems by Saadi

Cast

HASAN-ALI — A blacksmith in his 40s; strong build, focused, and determined.

MAHMOUD — In his teens; a servant to Dervish Ali, worldy-wise but good at heart..

SCHOOLTEACHER — In late 20s, confident and well groomed, very strict in the classroom.

SAJA — A girl between the ages of 10 to 13; lively, ambitious, eager to learn and obtain knowledge.

PACKSADDLE MAKER — A man in his 30s; Saja's father, submissive and serious.

BUSHRA — A baker in her 40s; strong-willed, disciplined, lively, likes to try new things.

MASTER JAFAR — A builder in his 40s. He has a "measure twice, cut once" personality, meaning he wants copious instructions for things outside his domain of expertise, but he is take-charge and confident with anything concerning construction.

KHADIJA	A carpet weaver in her 60s; gentle, shy, nervous, pays attention to detail.
MINISTER OF THE CULTURAL OFFICE	Typical bureaucrat, obsessed with rules and protocol, very formal.

Extras: SCHOOLDCHILDREN; APPRENTICES TO BAKER, BUILDER, CARPET WEAVER

Production Notes:

All scenes take place in the village. At end of play, Master Jafar and his assistants build a simple platform (for the awards ceremony) on the stage.

Scene 1. Main street of a Persian village circa early 19th century. School in corner. Bakery, Carpet maker, builder, and other shop fronts.

Artisans and their apprentices are sitting in shops doing work. In school, SCHOOLTEACHER, SAJA, *and* SCHOOLCHILDREN *pantomime lesson.*

Enter HASAN-ALI *mopping his forehead. He walks quickly to the Dervish's door and knocks.* MAHMOUD *opens door and steps onstage.*

HASAN-ALI: Peace be upon you. May I speak with Dervish Ali?

MAHMOUD: Peace be upon you, too. The Dervish is not available.

HASAN-ALI: Writing his poetry, is he?

MAHMOUD: Actually, he is out in the field, harvesting his crops. He won't be back until sundown. By then he will be quite tired. What do you want of him?

HASAN-ALI: My neighbor is going to Mashhad, where my son lives. I wanted my neighbor to give my son a letter, and normally the grocer writes the letter for me, but today he was out. Then I came here to the Dervish, but he is out. I don't know who can help me.

MAHMOUD: You can't write yourself?

HASAN-ALI *shakes head sadly*.

MAHMOUD: Perhaps you could try the school? Maybe the teacher could write the letter.

HASAN-ALI: Brilliant idea! Blessings upon you, brother!

MAHMOUD: And on you. *(Closes door.)*

HASAN-ALI *runs to school. Knocks on door.*

SCHOOLTEACHER: What is it?

HASAN-ALI: Begging your pardon; may I have permission to enter the classroom?

SCHOOLTEACHER: Very well. Peace be upon you.

ALL SCHOOLCHILDREN: Peace be upon you.

HASAN-ALI: And peace be on all of you, too. Excellency, I don't want to give you any trouble, but my neighbor is departing for Mashhad shortly, and I need to write a few words to my son. The grocer or Dervish Ali usually helps me write, but neither of them is around. Please, I beg you, please write a short letter for me, and I'll give you anything you wish.

SCHOOLTEACHER: I have to teach now. If the school were closed, I'd be happy to help you, but I myself can't do it right now. *(Calls to student.)* Saja, go over to that corner, and write a letter for Hasan-Ali.

HASAN-ALI *and* SAJA *sit together in corner.* As HASAN-ALI *speaks,* SAJA *writes down his words.*

HASAN-ALI: Son, I need you to get me a new emery wheel, a new fuller, and some of the new wax from Merv. Now that wax might be hard to get, but I'd like to try it out. *(To Saja.)* Are you getting all this?

SAJA: Yes, sir. What is your son's name?

HASAN-ALI: Haroon. Let's see. Also, send everything with this same caravan; they will come back through the village in two months. The caravaneer is very reliable. I'm giving him a packsaddle; put everything in the packsaddle. Did you write everything down just as I said it?

SAJA: Let me read it to you. Listen and see if I missed anything. *(Reads from letter.)* "My beloved son Haroon, how are you and your family? We hear Mashhad is beautiful this time of year. Your mother and I are in good health, but we miss you. Using your excellent judgment, could you please select for me these items: 1) an emery wheel, 2) a fuller, and 3) wax from Merv, if you can obtain it. I have given the caravaneer a packsaddle; please put all the items in the pack and the caravaneer will deliver it to me forthwith. Please give my love to your wife and the children. Your father Hasan-Ali."

HASAN-ALI: That is a wonderful letter! I am very pleased. How can such a small girl as you be so educated? Did you learn everything in this school?

SAJA: Of course. No one else in my family knows how to write. I've learned to read and write from our teacher. I've taught my sister at home what I've learned here, but I've a long way to go before I become really educated.

HASAN-ALI: No, you write better than I do. Bravo and bless you, for you are very educated!

SAJA *and* HASAN-ALI *go to the teacher. On the way,* HASAN-ALI *knocks over a stool. He apologizes and tries to put the stool upright.*

HASAN-ALI: *(To* SCHOOLTEACHER.*)* Thank you very much. You and your student have helped me a great deal. I have something I need to talk with you about. With your permission, I'll come to you in the afternoon when the school is closed.

SCHOOLTEACHER: Very well. May I see the letter?

HASAN-ALI *hands him the letter.*

SCHOOLTEACHER: Well done! Saja has a good handwriting.

SAJA *bows head modestly and returns to her seat.*

HASAN-ALI: Good-bye.

ALL SCHOOLCHILDREN: Good-bye.

HASAN-ALI *leaves school and starts to walk back to his shop.*

HASAN-ALI: That Saja, such a little girl, but she wrote such a fine letter that even the teacher praised her work! How many years has she been studying? As far as I know, Saja is the daughter of the packsaddle maker at the other end of the quarter. It seems just like yesterday that she was a tiny tot playing in the streets. How long has she been going school? A year? Less than that? So, if I'd been going to school for a year or a little less, I'd know how to read and write. Am I less than a small child?

Exit HASAN-ALI.

School bell rings; children shout and run out of class. SCHOOLTEACHER *sorts papers. Enter* HASAN-ALI *carrying a paper cone filled with rock candy. He knocks on door to the school.*

SCHOOLTEACHER: Enter. Peace be upon you, brother blacksmith.

HASAN-ALI: And Peace on you, too, Excellency. This is for the letter that I gave you trouble about. (*Hands him the cone of candy.*)

SCHOOLTEACHER: Why, thank you, but this wasn't necessary.

HASAN-ALI: Dear sir, I've come to you to ask you something. Is it only children who can learn to read and write? Can older people learn too?

SCHOOLTEACHER: Anyone can learn to read and write. In fact, some older people can do it faster than children.

HASAN-ALI: Faster?

SCHOOLTEACHER: Yes, faster. Children are sometimes not very motivated go to school. Their parents make them go. We have to work very hard to get them interested in their lessons. When they study, they still don't understand that it will be useful to them later in life. They play around and waste time, but an adult who wants to learn to read and write gives it more importance and works harder to learn.

HASAN-ALI: Today I have decided to learn to read and write, but I have to work in my shop during the daytime, and I can't come to school then. Would it be possible for me to come in the evenings and learn from you?

SCHOOLTEACHER: The day school is for children, and I spend my evenings reading books. By the end of the day, I don't have the strength to do any more teaching.

HASAN-ALI: But I can pay for the lessons.

SCHOOLTEACHER: I don't object to work and earning money, but I can't do everything. Honestly, at the end of the day I am exhausted. Look, my plan is when there are a lot of children in the village who know how to read and write, then each one of them can teach a few others. Gradually, over the years, everyone in the village will know how to read and write.

HASAN-ALI: That is a clever plan.

SCHOOLTEACHER: You know the saying, "Even if you know the Day of Judgment is tomorrow, don't hesitate to plant the date palm seed." *(*HASAN-ALI *looks confused.)* Do what you can while you can. (HASAN-ALI *pretends to understand.*) We have an example: Saja, daughter of the packsaddle maker, and the one who helped you. She taught her little sister to read and write, and her handwriting is even better!

HASAN-ALI: I like your plan, with the village children and all, but it takes so long. *(Disappointed.)* Isn't there any way a person can learn to read and write in one day?

SCHOOLTEACHER: *(Laughing.)* No, there isn't. Could you become a blacksmith in one day? Of course not, and the same is true for education. You can't become educated in one day, not by prayers, or vows, or pleas, or money, or force, or eagerness, no matter how much! A person has to spend several months or a year doing it. It takes time, concentration, and memory.

HASAN-ALI: I knew it would be hard. That's why I've always hesitated.

SCHOOLTEACHER: Hasan-Ali, it may be hard, but becoming educated is a worthy goal! Reading and writing are the foundation of knowledge. The poet Saadi tells us, "Every leaf of the tree becomes a page of the sacred scripture once the soul has learnt to read." Yes, it may be difficult, but the path to knowledge is the same for all people.

HASAN-ALI: The path to knowledge is the same for everyone? Time, concentration, and memory? *(*SCHOOLTEACHER *nods.)*

SCHOOLTEACHER: There are a lot of things you can buy with money, or get by force, or pray for, but you have to pursue knowledge all on your own. Whoever studies most and best learns most and best. Even if you own the entire world, you cannot become educated without hard work. Are you afraid of hard work?

HASAN-ALI: Excellency, I am a blacksmith. I have never been afraid of hard work. But there are short cuts. What about the naked poet, Baba Taher?

SCHOOLTEACHER: Naked? Taher is a famous poet; why do you talk of him being naked?

HASAN-ALI: I heard a story. Everyone in Taher's village made fun of him because he couldn't read or write. He became very sad, and then he asked a scholar how to become educated. The scholar told him, "You must break the ice of the pool in the schoolyard and bathe in the frozen water." So he did it, and that ice bath made him educated in one night! All that education made him a famous poet!

SCHOOLTEACHER: You can listen to these tall stories, but believing them is a different matter! Yes, Taher was a famous poet; it is true. You can see his tomb in Hamadan today, and his poems are loved by most people who speak Persian. But he either was illiterate and had a God-given talent to create poetry, or he had taken the pains to learn to read and write. Certainly he didn't become educated in one night!

HASAN-ALI: No naked ice bath shortcut?

SCHOOLTEACHER: No. No shortcuts. Just hard work. You must keep your clothes on at all times while learning!

HASAN-ALI: Then why do people tell such lies?

SCHOOLTEACHER: Don't be so hard on storytellers. What probably happened is someone figured out that many people enjoy marvelous tales. Taher's fans wanted to increase his importance, so they tell such stories about him and probably hope that more people will read his poems. There are hundreds of such miraculous stories about sufis and dervishes, but most of them aren't true.

HASAN-ALI: Then how …?

SCHOOLTEACHER: *(Shrugging.)* Perhaps Taher had an exceptionally good memory and learned quickly what he heard. If he could read and write, I'm certain that he learned to do so the way the rest of us do, by lessons and practice. There are no shortcuts to knowledge.

HASAN-ALI: *(Convinced.)* All right. Now tell me what I should do. I want to learn to read and write. If I can find someone to teach me, how long do you think it will take me?

SCHOOLTEACHER: That depends on your ability, eagerness, and your determination. One person can learn in three months, but another will take longer. Just about everyone can learn to read and write within a year. You could, for example, study with that Saja in the evenings, and after a while you'll be able to read and write to your heart's content.

HASAN-ALI: Are you saying that even Saja can make me educated?

SCHOOLTEACHER: Yes, why not? Didn't I tell you that she had taught her little sister? Don't you have the ability of a little 6-year-old girl?

HASAN-ALI: Certainly, but …

SCHOOLTEACHER: Your own son learned blacksmithing from you, correct?

HASAN-ALI: Yes, I taught him everything he knows!

SCHOOLTEACHER: Well, can't your son teach the blacksmithing trade to someone else? He can teach as much as he knows, be it a little or a lot. That Saja we've been talking about can read books very well, but the more she reads, the better she'll become.

HASAN-ALI: You've made me very happy. You've put me on the right track. If I can learn to write letters, that will be an accomplishment for me. Thank you very much. Peace and blessings upon you, and God be with you!

SCHOOLTEACHER: God be with you.

HASAN-ALI *leaves the school and walks over to the house of the packsaddle maker and knocks at his door. Enter* PACKSADDLE MAKER.

HASAN-ALI: Peace be upon you, brother.

PACKSADDLE MAKER: And peace be upon you, brother.

HASAN-ALI: I was just speaking to the schoolmaster this evening about education. I want to learn how to read and write.

PACKSADDLE MAKER: A worthy endeavor!

HASAN-ALI: Indeed. Unfortunately, our schoolmaster does not have time in the evenings to teach me. He's a busy fellow. He suggested that your daughter, Saja, teach me.

PACKSADDLE MAKER: *(Surprised.)* Saja? But she is just a girl.

HASAN-ALI: True, but the schoolmaster is very impressed by her abilities. What do you say?

PACKSADDLE MAKER: There's nothing that I can say, friend. Personally, I'm very happy when I watch my Saja reading books and writing things, but I work hard from dawn to dusk for the welfare of my family. I can't order Saja to spend her evenings giving you lessons unless she wants to do it herself.

HASAN-ALI: May I ask her?

PACKSADDLE MAKER: Yes, but if she should agree, you'll have to come here.

HASAN-ALI: Whatever you say. I've got to learn to read and write. The schoolmaster said that it wasn't too difficult. But even if it is, I'm ready to tackle it!

PACKSADDLE MAKER: Saja, come here.

Enter SAJA.

SAJA: Peace be upon you, Brother blacksmith.

HASAN-ALI: And peace on you, Saja.

PACKSADDLE MAKER: Brother Hasan-Ali here wants to learn to read and write. Your schoolteacher recommended you for the job. Would you be willing to teach him what you know in the evenings?

SAJA: I have to study my lessons during the day, and the rest of the time I play and read more books. If I teach in the evenings, I won't have time to do those things I enjoy. My time is valuable.

HASAN-ALI: I understand this will take your time, but all my life I have wondered what it would be like to read and write. Now I am at an age where I find that I need to be able to write, especially since my son lives in a different town.

PACKSADDLE MAKER: Pursing knowledge is a worthy goal. In the case of Hasan-Ali, it will also benefit his whole family. Your teacher recommended you Saja; think it over.

SAJA: Very well, father.

Pause while SAJA *thinks it over.* HASAN-ALI *accidentally knocks over a metal water pitcher; he apologizes profusely.*

SAJA: I've thought it over, and I've prepared a plan. If you agree, I'll do it. If not …Well, that's up to you. *(Pauses.)* I'm not going to teach in the evenings unless there is some greater benefit. I don't want to teach just one person. If Brother Hasan-Ali can get four more people who are ready to learn to read and write in the evening, I'll open an evening school here, just as the teacher has a day school. I'll teach all of you as much as I know, and you will all be able to read books and write anything you want to. In addition to five students, there are three conditions that must be met. It you meet my conditions, then there is one great benefit.

HASAN-ALI: I can find four people, but what are your conditions? Not everyone can pay money.

SAJA: *(Shocked.)* Money? I don't want any money. The three conditions are these: First, my father must be one of the students and be present in class. Second, I won't teach an unskilled person. My father is a packsaddle maker. You're a blacksmith. The other three must be skilled workers, such as carpenters, painters, tailors, shoemakers, people like that. Third, with the exception of my father, the other students must agree that in exchange for the lessons I give, they will teach me anything I want to know about their trades. Of course, I'll promise that I won't spend any more time learning from them than I use teaching them.

HASAN-ALI: Well that's not so bad. In fact, that's quite good! Very Good! You've spoken well. I pray that you may always prosper! I'll find the other students, and I approve of your conditions. But what is this great benefit you spoke of?

SAJA: The great benefit is that I'll make the five of you able to read and write in the space of a single month!

HASAN-ALI: In one month? Wonderful!

SAJA: Yes, one month. Or, to be more exact, 32 days.

PACKSADDLE MAKER: What are you saying daughter? You can't do it in such a short time!

SAJA: Why can't I? What do they want to know? They want to be able to write what is said in our own Persian tongue. That is the key to literacy. When the blacksmith Hasan-Ali is able to write all that he says, when he wants to write "peace" or "be quiet," then it will be his choice what to write. That is all the education he is asking for.

HASAN-ALI: That's just what I want.

SAJA: He can choose whether he wants to read more and learn more or if he is simply satisfied with writing short letters.

HASAN-ALI: If I can write everything I can say, that'll be enough for me!

SAJA: You think it'll be enough now. Afterward you'll see that the more you read, the more you'll understand, and the more you will want to know. A little arithmetic and geometry is also handy. In any case, I'll put the key of education in your hands. It is your choice how to use it.

HASAN-ALI: When can we start?

SAJA: You know the terms for my school. Assemble the students, then report back to me. Peace be upon you Brother Hasan-Ali. *(Makes a short bow to both men.)* Father. (PACKSADDLE MAKER *motions to* SAJA *that she is free to leave.*)

HASAN-ALI: Peace and blessings upon you, Saja.

Exit SAJA.

HASAN-ALI: *(Turns to* PACKSADDLE MAKER.*)* So, your daughter wants you to learn how to read and write.

PACKSADDLE MAKER: Yes, it appears that she does.

HASAN-ALI: This is a wonderful opportunity for you! All this education right under your own roof.

PACKSADDLE MAKER: Yes, indeed. *(Uncomfortable silence.)*

HASAN-ALI: Why do you hesitate, man? I need you if I am going to have my night school.

PACKSADDLE MAKER: It's just a little embarrassing to be taught by my own child. It's not the natural order of things.

HASAN-ALI: Look brother, sometimes in order to get the greatest rewards, we have to humble ourselves. Do you think it will be easy for me, a big strong fellow, to be taught by some snippet of a girl? Of course not, but look at the big reward. From this small girl, we are going to get the gift of education.

PACKSADDLE MAKER: True.

HASAN-ALI: Don't you think it is worth it, a little humbleness now for greater knowledge later?

PACKSADDLE MAKER: You've convinced me Hasan-Ali; I will be my daughter's student.

HASAN-ALI: Peace and blessings on you brother! Now I need to find three more students for the night school. God be with you!

PACKSADDLE MAKER: And with you!

Lights dim.

Scene 2. The next afternoon.

HASAN-ALI *does a pantomime going into the market place, knocking on doors, explaining to people about the school. Some shake their heads "no," but eventually he finds three students*: MASTER JAFAR, BUSHRA, *and* KHADIJA. *They all walk to the packsaddle maker's house and knock on the door.* PACKSADDLE MAKER *answers and greets them. In the meantime,* SAJA *has been putting together her "schoolroom."* SAJA *turns to her father and the other adults.*

HASAN-ALI: I've done as you asked and found students for the class. There is your esteemed father, myself, Hasan-Ali the blacksmith, and now may I introduce Bushra, the baker, *(*BUSHRA *hands* SAJA *a loaf of bread)* Master Jafar, the builder, *(he hands* SAJA *a small wooden house)* and Khadija, the carpet weaver *(*KHADIJA *gives* SAJA *a small carpet).* Please sit here. *(Gestures to the ground in front of the paper pad. He claps his hands together.)* We are here and eager to learn. *(He sits down.)*

SAJA *begins her lesson the same way she has seen his teacher start his class. She passes out a slate and chalk to each student, then stands at the front of the classroom.*

SAJA: Well students, pay attention. You're no longer children, and now is not the time to play. You've come to school to learn to read and write. You know what you want to do. So, pay attention and everyone must study. Now, I have some questions. *(Turns to* HASAN-ALI*).* First, tell me: How many names of flowers and plants do you know?

HASAN-ALI: A lot, miss.

SAJA: *(To* BUSHRA*.)* How many names of people do you know that you're able to say?

BUSHRA: Lots, miss. Hundreds. Thousands!

SAJA: *(Turns to* MASTER JAFAR*.)* Very good. How many names of food and things you can eat do you know?

MASTER JAFAR: Many, miss! Everything. I know the names of everything I've eaten and even things that I haven't.

SAJA: Good. *(To* KHADIJA*.)* How many things that you do every day can you name? Such as standing, sitting, sleeping, getting up, going, returning, speaking?

KHADIJA: *(Laughing.)* I can make a string of lots of such things: Running, falling, eating, buying, selling, seeing, hearing, hitting, breaking, making ... There are lots of such things.

SAJA: All right. (*Turns to* HASAN-ALI.) Now when you want to say my name, what do you do?

HASAN-ALI: Nothing miss, I just say it!

SAJA: If you want to tell me to do something, such as to go or to come, what do you say?

HASAN-ALI: That's obvious! I say "go" or "come."

SAJA: Now class, we all know how to speak. Learning to read and write is no different. Everything we say, we can write. If it's already written, we read it. When you can write the names of the things we've been talking about and read them when they are written, you've become educated! *(Now becoming serious.)* Everything in the world has a name. Every action has a name. Some are short, like "rose." When you say it, you move your mouth only once. Rose. Now all of you say it: Rose.

ALL STUDENTS: Rose.

SAJA: Other words are long, like "cottonseed." You move your mouth three times to say "cottonseed." Say it.

ALL STUDENTS: Cottonseed.

SAJA: Our tongues and our mouths are what we use to pronounce words. We can talk about anything in God's world with them. *(Holds up a book.)* Paper doesn't have a mouth or tongue, but when you learn to read, you will find that a book can speak to you.

HASAN-ALI: How is a book going to talk to us when it doesn't have a mouth or a tongue?

SAJA: A pen is the tongue, and a piece of paper the mouth for the words we write and read. Just as we can say anything with our mouths, we can write anything on paper and then read it. In our Persian alphabet, we have 32 letters. With them, we can write all the words of our language and then read them back. Writing is a way of speaking. We learn to speak as children, and with the alphabet we make writing and reading easy. That's all literacy consists of: Learning the 32 letters of our alphabet. *(The students nod in comprehension.)* For the first few days, I'll teach you one letter a day. Then two a day until you've learned all 32 letters. Then we'll work together on writing and reading. After you have learned that, our work will be done! *(The students look very surprised that it seems so simple.)* Today is the first day, so we must learn one letter. That letter is Ba. Everyone say "B."

ALL STUDENTS: B.

SAJA: Whenever we write it in this way *(she writes letter on paper pad)* we pronounce it "B." When we see it in a word, we say "B." This is one of the 32 letters. When we've learned them all, we can write everything in the world. *(The students write the letter "Ba" on their slates.* SAJA *looks at their progress and nods with approval.)* That is our lesson for today. I've written 52 words on these pieces of paper. *(Hands out bits of paper to students.)* Your homework is to look at them and find as many "B"s as you can. You must also write the letter "Ba" 100 times on a piece of paper and bring it to the next lesson. Every book that you see will probably have lots of "B"s. Remember the sound of this letter.

Lights dim, but still visible is SAJA *teaching the class. She pantomimes teaching, flipping through a pad of paper with one Persian letter on it per sheet to indicate the flow of time. Spotlight brightens a bit.*

SAJA: Now we can take these letters and join them together to make words!

SAJA *demonstrates this on pad of paper. Students copy on their slates. Lights fade fully out.*

Scene 3. SAJA's house, one month later.

HASAN-ALI, BUSHRA, KHADIJA, MASTER JAFAR, and PACKSADDLE MAKER *are seated.*

HASAN-ALI: It is hard to imagine that in just one month I am now able to write a letter to my son. I am so pleased, and my son is proud of me, too!

KHADIJA: I can write to my niece to ask for that red dye from Agra. The color is so strong and bright!

BUSHRA: I wrote to my cousin for the purple cardamom seeds for my spring festival bread. Guess what. Just before class, someone on the latest caravan from Balkh dropped the seeds off at my shop!

SAJA *enters.*

SAJA: Peace be upon you students.

ALL: And peace be upon you, miss.

SAJA: It has now been a little more than a month. You all know how to read and write. The key to learning is now in your hands. The more you read, the more you write, the better you will become.

HASAN-ALI: I think I speak for all of us when I say that we are very pleased that we have become educated so quickly.

SAJA: Today you must fulfill your part of the bargain.

ALL STUDENTS: Our part of the bargain?

SAJA: Yes, now you will teach me. *(Hands out paper.)* Write a list of all the tools and things you use in your trades and bring the lists to me.

All students start writing except MASTER JAFAR.

MASTER JAFAR: I don't understand.

SAJA: What are the names of the tools you use to build a house?

MASTER JAFAR: Let's see. A trowel, plumb line, T-square, adze, shovel, mortarboard, pick.

SAJA: That's it! Now just write it all down! On the paper.

They hand SAJA *the lists of paper.*

SAJA: Now write the names of everything that you make with your tools.

MASTER JAFAR: What do you mean?

SAJA: What parts of a house are you able to make?

MASTER JAFAR: Mortar, foundations, wall, partition, roof, doorway, kitchen, stairs, bathroom ...

SAJA: Excellent, yes! Please write it down, Master Builder. When you are finished, hand me your lists.

Students give lists to SAJA.

SAJA: Now, write the names of all the materials that you use in your work

MASTER JAFAR: So I should write down earth, gypsum, lime, sand, cement, plaster, clay adobe, bricks, tiles, and stone?

SAJA: YES!

SAJA *gets the lists. She puts all the lists in a pile for each profession.*

SAJA: Now I am going to ask you some questions, and I want you to write an explanation of each word beside it. So Master Builder Jafar, what is a partition?

MASTER JAFAR: A partition is a kind of thin wall made of one thickness of bricks. The wall is made strong by the plaster or mortar used to hold them together.

SAJA: Very good. But what is mortar?

MASTER JAFAR: It can be thick mud, or something else like lime or cement that is soft and is used to hold adobe blocks, bricks, or stones together. It's very strong after it has dried.

SAJA: Excellent. Is there only one kind of partition, or are there many kinds?

Lights dim out.

Scene 4. Village.

Everyone is bustling with activity, sweeping and cleaning shop fronts; some street vendors start to sell things. MASTER JAFAR *and his apprentices are building a small platform in the middle of the village.* SCHOOLTEACHER *enters carrying a travel bag and books, He looks as though he has just arrived from a holiday. He looks confused. He stops* BUSHRA *and* KHADIJAH.

SCHOOLTEACHER: What is going on in this village? I've never seen anything like this before.

BUSHRA: A special visitor from the capitol is coming.

SCHOOLTEACHER: Visitor? Why?

KHADIJAH: The visitor is going to preside over a big awards ceremony.

SCHOOLTEACHER: Just who is this visitor, and why is he giving out awards?

BUSHRA: It is the Minister of Culture.

SCHOOLTEACHER: Minister of Culture? To this village? Is this some kind of joke?

KHADIJAH: Oh, it's no joke. This is all Saja's work.

SCHOOLTEACHER: Saja?

KHADIJAH: Yes, Saja taught us to read and write, and in return we, her artisan students, gave her all kinds of information about our trades.

BUSHRA: Special information. She wrote everything down in that notebook of hers.

KHADIJAH: Saja wrote down all the words, jargon, tools, and materials for five trades in separate notebooks. When anyone drew pictures of things or plans, she copied them too.

BUSHRA: Then she took these notebooks, bound them up, and sent them to the Ministry of Culture in the capitol. Five books, can you imagine?

KHADIJAH: Saja says that our work is a historical record!

SCHOOLTEACHER: I can't believe what I am hearing! This is tremendous. The poet Rumi wrote, "When knowledge is lacking in a man's nature, His soul is like a stone on the plain." Saja has taken stones and used them to cultivate a garden!

KHADIJA *and* BUSHRA *look at each other quizzically, not sure how to take this backhanded compliment.*

The Awards Ceremony begins. Enter someone playing a horn, followed by the MINISTER OF CULTURE *and* SAJA *dressed in academic robes. The* MINISTER OF CULTURE *goes to the center of the podium;* SAJA *stands on his left side. The people in the village gather around. Another person brings in medals and books and sets them on the stage.*

MINISTER OF CULTURE: Peace be upon all of you! Welcome, citizens, welcome! We are very honored to be in your village today. For today, we are about to bestow a very unique award on a scholar and her collaborators, citizens born and bred in this very village! *(Applause.)* This scholar and her citizen collaborators are the very first to write down all the words about the things and materials that are used in their trades. Never before have we seen such comprehensive and detailed compilations. *(Applause.)* These written records are legacies of knowledge for those who come after us. These books have the benefit of experience and give us great knowledge of each profession. In the future, when jobs will be quite different from ours today, people will be able to read about our workers and learn what it was like and what they did. May the authors be blessed for their contributions! Please come forward to accept your award! *(The person who brought out the medals and books holds up one of the books high in the air for the crowd to see.)*
"A Dictionary of Building and Construction," by Saja Palanduz, with the help of Master Jafar, the master builder. *(Gives medal to* SAJA *and medal to* MASTER JAFAR. *Shakes their hands.)*
"A Dictionary of Packsaddle Making," by Saja Palanduz, with the help of her father, the Master Packsaddle Maker. *(Same medal presentation.)*
"A Dictionary of Baking," by Saja Palanduz, with the help of Bushra, the master baker. *(Same medal presentation.)*
"A Dictionary of Blacksmithing" by Saja Palanduz, with the help of Hasan-Ali, the master blacksmith. *(Same medal presentation.)*
"A Dictionary of Carpet Weaving," by Saja Palanduz, with the help of Khadija, master carpet weaver. *(Same medal presentation)*. This concludes our medal presentation ceremony; please join us for some delicious pomegranate juice to celebrate this historic achievement.

Two servers come in with drinks on a tray; the crowd takes the drinks. There is much mingling and congratulating awardees. SAJA *and* MAHMOUD *come to the front of the stage, glasses in hand.*

MAHMOUD: Saja, now that you have become famous and write books and receive honors, change your name. Pick a nicer name than Palanduz.

SAJA: Do you know what Palanduz means?

MAHMOUD: It means "packsaddle maker," right?

SAJA: Indeed yes, but I will not change my name. There are many nice and useless names. The importance of a name is not in its beauty. Palanduz is a good family name, and I am working so that everyone will respect it. Consider Omar Khayyam. What does Khayyam mean?

MAHMOUD: I haven't a clue.

SAJA: It means "tentmaker!" What about the great poet Attar?

MAHMOUD *shrugs his shoulders.*

SAJA: Perfume maker! It might as well be Baqqal: grocer! Greatness and honor is not in the beauty of the name. It's in good works. If my work is of any value, the name of Palanduz will be respected. People will say, "Bravo Saja Palanduz!" But if a person's work is no good, the most beautiful name in the world won't be worth a penny.

MAHMOUD: Bravo, Saja Palanduz!

SAJA: Thank you. Now I need to go and find more students! I have more books to write!

The End

A Lion Without a Mane or a Tail

Based on a poem by Rumi

Cast

NUHAID	Big, athletic, not terribly intelligent, cowardly; his names means "big" in Arabic.
LITTLE ALI	Skinny, curious, animated, likes to talk.
TATTOOER	Tries very hard to be pleasing and polite. He starts out patient but gets increasingly more and more frustrated until he completely loses his temper at the end.

Setting: Outside the TATTOOER's shop. LITTLE ALI and NUHAID are standing in front of the shop.

LITTLE ALI: Nuhaid, you are so big and strong. You lift those bags of wheat all day long and load them on the carts.

NUHAID: That's my job, Little Ali.

LITTLE ALI: Why are you in front of this shop?

NUHAID: I am going to get a tattoo.

LITTLE ALI: A tattoo? Why?

NUHAID: I want a tattoo to show people how strong and brave I am.

LITTLE ALI: But my mamma says that only thugs get tattoos on their arms, chests, and stomachs. She says that a lion or a leopard stands for bravery, a picture of a friend is a sign of loyalty, and a knife or sword means strength and fighting.

NUHAID: Your mother seems to know quite a lot about tattoos.

LITTLE ALI: So what kind of tattoo are you going to get?

NUHAID: Umm. Well. Hmmm. Animals are good. Which animal is the bravest animal of them all?

LITTLE ALI: The lion. For sure, the lion. He is king of the jungle, and you can only be king of the jungle if you are brave.

NUHAID: A lion it is then!

LITTLE ALI: My mamma says it hurts to get a tattoo. *(This is news to Nuhaid. He starts to quiver with fear.)* They poke you with a needle! *(*LITTLE ALI *starts poking* NUHAID *with his finger.)* Poke! Poke! I hate needles.

NUHAID: Little Ali, stop that poking. It's time for you to go to school now.

LITTLE ALI: I will go as long as I can be the first one to see your new tattoo!

NUHAID: We'll see. Now get moving!

Exit LITTLE ALI. *Enter* TATTOOER.

TATTOOER: Good day, sir, how may I help you?

NUHAID: Good day. I wish to get a tattoo.

TATTOOER: A big strong fellow such as yourself; a fine idea, my good sir. Now, what sort of picture would you like?

NUHAID: I'm an athlete, strong, and brave. I want a lion tattoo.

TATTOOER: A lion: Very good choice I might say. My lions are well regarded in the community. Very ferocious.

NUHAID: Ferocious?

TATTOOER: Fierce. You know, scary looking. (NUHAID *nods head enthusiastically.*) On what part of your body do you want your tattoo?

NUHAID: On my right arm, near the shoulder.

TATTOOER. Very good. Let us begin. First roll up your sleeve and sit down over there. *(*NUHAID *sits.)* First I will wash your skin with some water to make the surface clean. *(Washes* NUHAID's *arm with sponge.)*

NUHAID: Hey! That water is hot!

TATTOOER: Your dirt is tenacious.

NUHAID: What are you talking about?

TATTOOER: The dirt is sticking to you like flies on honey. (NUHAID *shrugs.*) Now I draw the picture lightly. (NUHAID *giggles.*) And now let's start the real thing. (TATTOOER *picks up tattoo needle and starts to prick* NUHAID's *skin.)*

NUHAID: Ouch! My arm! What are you doing?

TATTOOER: I'm doing what you asked me to do! Didn't you say you wanted the tattoo of a lion?

NUHAID: Of course. But, um, from what point are you starting?

TATTOOER: I started with the lion's tail. With the tip of the lion's tail.

NUHAID: You know what? For now, let's just forget about the tail and do the head and body. My lion won't have a tail. Let's suppose my lion's tail was cut off.

TATTOOER: No problem; we'll forget about the tail. *(Starts to prick skin with needle.)*

NUHAID: Yee-ouch! That hurts a lot! What are you doing?

TATTOOER: I'm making a lion. Relax a little, and I'll be through before you know it.

NUHAID: What part of the lion are you working on now?

TATTOOER: The mane.

NUHAID: Actually, the mane and neck aren't so important. How about my lion doesn't have a mane? The body will be enough.

TATTOOER: As you wish; we'll forget about the mane, too. *(To audience.)* I can't start from the tail, and I can't start from the head. Why don't I start from the feet? *(Pokes needle into* NUHAID's *arm.)*

NUHAID: Hoo wee mamma! Ouch-o-rama! What kind of a fussy worker are you? The paws can't be seen. I don't want an art gallery on my arm. All I want, very simple, is the shape of a lion.

TATTOOER: The shape of a lion?

NUHAID: Just a simple lion. Forget the paws. My lion doesn't have any feet. Now do something so it doesn't hurt so much, and hurry up and finish!

TATTOOER: Yes sir! From now on I'll just deal with the actual shape of the lion and forget about the details. *(Brings the needle to* NUHAID's *arm again.)*

NUHAID: Yi yi yi yi! You're killing me with that needle! What are you doing? What part of the lion are you working on?

TATTOOER: The most important part of the body of the lion, the stomach. There is no way to avoid it.

NUHAID: No, sir! My lion doesn't need a stomach. Do something so that there is a lion, but with no stomach.

TATTOOER: *(Thinks a minute, then throws down needle.)* Forgive me, mister champion athlete. I'm very sorry. Until now, I've tattooed a thousand men and have drawn the picture of a lion on a man's body a hundred times, but I have never seen a lion without a mane, or a tail, or a stomach! Who has ever seen a lion without a mane or a tail or a belly? When did God ever create such a lion? Since you can't put up with the pricks of the needle, it's better if you let your arm stay the way it is. Save me the bother, and stop pretending that you are a brave man and a lion-killer! Since you cannot endure the prick of the needle, stop talking about lions and fierce beasts!

The End

The Unfair Verdict

Based on a poem by Rumi

Cast
DOCTOR   Professional, thorough, cold.

OLD MAN   Sickly, may be slightly demented.

DERVISH   Temperamental, outwardly spiritual, but inwardly turbulent.

JUDGE   Diplomatic, interested in following the rules unless it is politically expedient not to do so.

Setting: In the far right is a DOCTOR's office, in the middle of the stage is a meadow, and on the far left stage is the JUDGE's house.

Opening scene, stage far right, DOCTOR's office. OLD MAN *is being examined by* DOCTOR.

OLD MAN: I haven't been feeling well for a long time. Please do something.

DOCTOR: *(Taking the pulse from different points on* OLD MAN*'s wrist.)* What did you eat last night?

OLD MAN: Nothing.

DOCTOR: *(Listening to his chest.)* Breathe in, out. What did you have for breakfast?

OLD MAN: Nothing.

DOCTOR: *(Looking at* OLD MAN*'s eyes, pulls down the lower lid.)* Say "Ahhhh."

OLD MAN: *(Sticks out tongue.)* Ahhhh.

DOCTOR: *(Examines tongue.)* Hold your hands in front of you and push down on my hands. (OLD MAN *does so.)* That's enough. You don't require any special diet or medicine. You need to eat more. To get better, you should do what you want to do. Eat anything you want, and do the things you enjoy. If you do that, your health will improve.

OLD MAN: This is a good plan, but I can't eat anything I want to eat. I don't have money to do that.

DOCTOR: Look, don't worry so much about these things. You should live out your dreams as much as you possibly can with what you do have.

OLD MAN: Live out my dreams?

DOCTOR: Yes! Follow your dreams! Live them! Eat as much as you can so that you have the energy to do what you feel like doing.

OLD MAN: God bless you, doctor! You have made me feel better already. My whims and wishes have never been realized, and now is the time to start making them come true!

DOCTOR: Yes, my good man! That's the spirit! May you be well and go wherever you want and make your dreams come true!

OLD MAN: Make my dreams come true! I want to go and look at meadows and flowing water.

DOCTOR: Excellent plan. There is a beautiful field and a small stream not far from my office. Just keep to the right when you leave. Go in good health!

OLD MAN: Thank you, and Peace be upon you!

OLD MAN *exits* DOCTOR*'s office and goes outside to meadow (center stage). He sees the* DERVISH *sitting on the riverbank, bent over and washing his hands, arms, and face. The* DERVISH *does not notice the* OLD MAN. OLD MAN *comes up behind the* DERVISH.

OLD MAN: His neck is so clean and smooth! The perfect spot for a slap. Now I shouldn't hit another man without reason, but the doctor says I should do whatever I want. Live out my dreams, and this will be the remedy for what ails me.

OLD MAN *rolls up sleeve, gets closer, and slaps* DERVISH *hard on the back of the neck. The* DERVISH *nearly falls into the river. He jumps up.*

DERVISH: *(Shouting.)* Hey! What's going on?

OLD MAN *starts laughing.* DERVISH *sees the* OLD MAN, *and even though he wants to beat him, he realizes the man is very sick, and if he takes his revenge he might kill the* OLD MAN. *He seizes the wrist of the* OLD MAN.

DERVISH: Wretch! Don't you want to keep your head on your body? Why did you hit me? I was minding my own business. I wasn't provoking you. You haven't got the strength to hit me hard, and you are too weak for me to hit you back. Why did you hit me in the first place? Why are you laughing like that? Are you crazy?

OLD MAN: I don't know why I did it. I just felt the urge, and the doctor told me to do whatever I wanted. I was laughing because the slap made a strange sound, and I don't know whether it was from my hand or your neck.

DERVISH: You don't know? I'll explain it to you now.

DERVISH *drags* OLD MAN *by the wrist to the* JUDGE*'s house (stage far left) and knocks on* JUDGE*'s door.*

DERVISH: Open up! I need to see the Judge right away! Where is the Judge? Where is she? I have a complaint, and I demand justice now! Open up!

JUDGE *opens door and comes out.*

JUDGE: Calm down. What is all the fuss about?

DERVISH: I demand justice, and I need a fair verdict here. I was sitting by the river, washing my hands and face, minding my own business, when out of nowhere, I get a slap on the back of the neck. I turn around, and I see this old fool laughing his head off. He freely admits to slapping me and tells me the doctor gave him permission!

JUDGE: Is what he says true? (OLD MAN *nods.*) Do you own the meadow or the stream? (OLD MAN *shakes head "no."*) And you slapped this man for no reason?

OLD MAN: His neck was so clean and smooth. It was very slap-able. The doctor said I should do what I want to do to get better, live out my dreams. My dream was to hit his slap-able neck. So I did.

DERVISH: That is my complaint. Assault. Here is the culprit. (*Lets go of* OLD MAN's *wrist and pushes him towards the* JUDGE.) You are the judge. If you say that I should retaliate, then say so, and I'll do it. If not, what is to be done? I was afraid to hit him because he is so weak I might kill him. It isn't right that in a town where there is a judge that a man should strike another without cause.

JUDGE: *(To* DERVISH.) Friend, you can't hit this sick old man because he might really die, and then his blood would be on your head. Beating and imprisonment is for strong, healthy men, not for old sick men, such as he. He is barely alive as it is. Come; forgive him. They say that there is a pleasure in forgiveness that is not to be found in revenge. Forgiveness is appropriate in a situation like this.

DERVISH: Why should I forgive him? What sort of an unfair verdict are you delivering? If people hear about it, there will be no stopping anyone! For every crime, there must be a punishment. I'll never forgive him, not for 30 years! You must punish him!

JUDGE: Look, I already explained it to you. This man is ill. He's on the point of death. You must withdraw your complaint.

DERVISH: I'll never agree to such a thing.

JUDGE: *(To* OLD MAN.*)* How much money do you have?

OLD MAN: Nothing.

JUDGE: What did you eat this morning?

OLD MAN: Nothing.

JUDGE: *(To* Dervish.*)* Do you see? He's also hungry! His slap hasn't taken anything from you. Let him go. How much money do you have?

DERVISH: Six copper coins.

JUDGE: Good, divide the money in half and give three coppers to this sick man so he can go and get something to eat. God will reward you for it.

DERVISH: This is justice? I am slapped by an old man, and then I have to pay him? This is completely unjust! It's tyranny and taxation. What kind of lousy judgment are you giving? How much does each slap cost?

JUDGE *and* DERVISH *start to argue.*

OLD MAN: *(To audience.)* It's clear that one slap is worth three coppers. *(He looks at the* JUDGE's *neck.)* The judge's neck is brighter, smoother, and nicer than the Dervish's neck. (OLD

MAN *slaps the* JUDGE's *neck.* JUDGE *falls down on the floor.*) Now you give me three coppers, too, to make things even!

DERVISH: *(Laughing really hard, he takes out all his money and gives it to the* JUDGE.) Take it all. Three coppers for the blow he struck on me and three for the blow he struck on you.

JUDGE: *(Getting up, rubbing her neck.)* What are you saying? Are you paying to have me beaten?

DERVISH: Yes. If a slap on the neck is right for one, it is right for all. If it is wrong for one, it is wrong for all. It's too bad I don't have any more money on me. If I had, I would have paid a hundred copper coins for him to hit you again! That would be right and just for such an unfair verdict! Then you might learn that whatever you don't approve of for yourself, you shouldn't approve of for others!

JUDGE: Alright Dervish, you have a point. Even though I don't approve of your lifestyle, you speak justly.

DERVISH: What's wrong with my lifestyle?

JUDGE: You travel too much. You need to settle down and grow some roots.

DERVISH: What is the point of having roots when you can't see the injustice in your town? Why is this old, sick man so thin and hungry?

OLD MAN *starts to sniff the air.*

OLD MAN: What is that wonderful smell?

JUDGE: *(Proudly.)* That is my husband's famous onion soup. Please, both of you, be my guests and try out the delicious onion soup. I only have one rule.

OLD MAN *and* DERVISH: What's that?

JUDGE: No hitting!

The End

The Old Woman's Cat

<u>CAST</u>
NARRATOR
OLD WOMAN
CAT
PALACE CAT
COOK
SCULLERY MAID

NARRATOR: There once was an old woman who lived in a rundown house. She had a skinny, sickly cat. It never went outside the house to look for food because as a kitten, children had frightened it, and a dog had chased it.

CAT: What is that wonderful smell coming from the neighbor's house?

OLD WOMAN: That's meat kabobs. But we can't afford such luxuries. Here is some bread, and you can have a bit of my soup.

CAT: Thank you, mistress.

OLD WOMAN: What is that sound I hear in the walls?

CAT: That is a mouse! Yeah! Maybe I can have a mouse for my dinner.

NARRATOR: The cat would sit by a hole in the wall hoping that a mouse would come out so it could catch it. A mouse was the only delicious morsel the cat would ever taste. One day the thin cat climbed up to the roof of the house and sniffed at the food that was being cooked in the city.

CAT: What is that powerful animal I see on the neighbor's roof? It has such long whiskers! Oh no! He's coming this way! I will never be able to escape from such a strong creature.

PALACE CAT: Hey, you there.

CAT: *(Scared.)* Yes? *(Surprised.)* Oh my, are you a cat, too?

PALACE CAT: Yes, of course I'm a cat. Why did you think I would be anything else?

CAT: I've never seen such a strong, beautiful cat before. May I ask: How did you get to be so big and strong?

PALACE CAT: Thank you for your kind words. When I first saw you, because you were so skinny, I thought you were a spider.

CAT: I'm not a spider!

PALACE CAT: Yes, I can see that now. You are indeed, a cat. A skinny cat, but still a cat.

CAT: So what is your secret to being so healthy?

PALACE CAT: The reason I am so big and strong is because I enjoy life. I eat well, I sleep well, and I enjoy myself as much as I can. That's how I became so fat and fit!

CAT: What do you eat? Where do you get your food?

PALACE CAT: I eat the crumbs from the sultan's table. I go to the sultan's kitchen every day and eat some fresh bread and butter with roast chicken and lamb kebab, and I am full until the next day. The rest of the time I play, enjoy myself, and rest.

CAT: That sounds like a great life.

PALACE CAT: Don't you know that food makes one fat? What did you think I did, gulp air? Blow myself up like a balloon? If you were to live as I do, eat all that delicious food, then you would become like me.

CAT: You're right. But the things you are talking about! I've never heard of roast chicken or seen a lamb kabob.

PALACE CAT: What do you eat?

CAT: Plain bread and sometimes a little of the old woman's soup. Once in a while, I catch a mouse.

PALACE CAT: *(Laughing.)* No wonder you are so weak and thin. What kind of a meal is a mouse? A mouse is only good for kittens to play with. In my opinion, you'd better do something for yourself. Life is short, and you should enjoy it as much as possible. Eat everything you can from any place.

CAT: I don't understand. If you eat from any place, who is your master?

PALACE CAT: I have no master! A noteworthy cat is one who doesn't stay in just one house but goes everywhere and eats the best foods.

CAT: But what about friendship? What about catching mice?

PALACE CAT: Look at what your friendship with the old woman has gotten you: You catch her mice and then are satisfied with bread and soup! If news of this gets out, your behavior will be a source of shame in the world of cats!

CAT: Great friend, now that you have opened my eyes, I too have hopes. Out of kindness to a fellow cat, will you tell me how to get to the sultan's kitchen so that I can fill my stomach there? If you do, I shall pray for your well being for the rest of my life.

PALACE CAT: I feel sorry for you. Meet me tomorrow morning on this roof, and I will take you to the sultan's kitchen.

CAT: Agreed!

NARRATOR: The cats said goodbye to each other and went their separate ways. The promise of the palace cat gave new life to the old woman's cat, and it returned home and told the old woman about the conversation with the palace cat.

OLD WOMAN: From what you have told me, it sounds as though this big cat is a shameless trickster who never catches mice and doesn't help its master.

CAT: Actually, he was quite friendly to me.

OLD WOMAN: That cat only knows how to fill its own stomach by stealing food from the sultan's kitchen.

CAT: But, the sultan has some great food. Roast chicken! Yum.

OLD WOMAN: But, it's stealing! Mark my words: It won't come to a good end! Take my advice and be satisfied with our calm, simple life. Wherever there is roast chicken, there is also danger. Our lives are not bad, and we have peace of mind.

CAT: What you say is true, but I can't just eat bread and soup. I hunger for roast chicken and lamb kabobs. We never have anything like that in this house. And now that I have found a cat that will get them for me, you won't let me! What a selfish old woman you are!

OLD WOMAN: My dear, your words are the words of inexperience. That cat that is going to get you roast chicken is not your friend. It's a trickster and beggar. No respectable person would let that cat into its house.

CAT: How can you say that about my new best friend?

OLD WOMAN: That cat lives by stealing: People don't cook roast chicken and lamb kabobs for cats! And the person who cooks that fancy food won't give it away freely. If you have any friend who wishes well for you, it is I. I've raised you and keep you close beside me. Well, I've had my say. Do what you will.

CAT: You watch me. I will have roast chicken and lamb kabob! And I will enjoy eating them!

NARRATOR: The desire for fancy food had overcome the cat's caution, and it did not pay attention to the old woman's advice. The next day, it followed the big cat to the sultan's kitchen. The cats did not know that the kitchen staff was in a very bad mood.

COOK: Those tricky cats! I work hard to cook delicious roast chicken and lamb kabob for the sultan, and then some cat comes along and steals all the food!

SCULLERY MAID: I am tired of chasing these cats around the kitchen. I am supposed to be washing dishes, not chasing cats.

COOK: The next time I catch a cat with a choice piece of meat, that cat is going to be in trouble!

SCULLERY MAID: We need to set a trap.

COOK: Good idea. Let's pile the meat in that corner, and then we'll hide.

SCULLERY MAID: Sounds like a good plan to me.

NARRATOR: The cats knew nothing of the trap.

PALACE CAT: Well, here is the place, the sultan's kitchen.

CAT: What is that delicious smell?

PALACE CAT: That is the smell of roast chicken and lamb kabob.

CAT: My mouth can hardly wait; let's go.

PALACE CAT: You know, I had a wonderful breakfast this morning, and I am not very hungry now. But you go ahead, eat your fill.

NARRATOR: The Old Woman's cat threw all caution to the wind. He ran into the kitchen and raced to the pile of meat in the corner of the kitchen. It had not reached the meat before …

COOK: Take that, you thief!

NARRATOR: The cook threw a kabob stick at the cat and hit it in the foot.

CAT: Ouch!

COOK: Gotcha!

SCULLERY MAID: I'll catch that thief! His hurt foot will slow him down. The cat will be punished for stealing!

CAT: I've got to get out of this crazy kitchen!
NARRATOR: The cat managed to escape from the sultan's kitchen and limped home dragging its foot.

OLD WOMAN: Let me bandage your paw for you, poor cat.

CAT: I promise I'll never listen to the trickster cats again. I'll never put myself in danger for a morsel of free food. I know now the value of the life I already have.

The End

The Ailing Eyes

CAST
MAN
DOCTOR

MAN: Ouch! Ouch! My stomach really hurts. I hope this doctor will see me.

DOCTOR: Hello, sir. What seems to be the problem?

MAN: Doctor, my stomach is giving me a lot of pain.

DOCTOR: How bad is your pain, sir?

MAN: I can't sleep. I need some medicine.

DOCTOR: Let me take your pulse. Hmm, seems fine. Let's have a look at your tongue.

MAN: *(Opening mouth.)* Ahhhhhh.

DOCTOR: That seems fine, too. Have you had this stomach pain for a long time?

MAN: No. This is the first time. It's never happened before.

DOCTOR: Has something happened to your stomach?

MAN: No. The trouble started half an hour after I ate supper, and it hasn't stopped hurting since.

DOCTOR: What did you eat before the pain started?

MAN: Some burnt toast. Nothing else.

DOCTOR: Are you sure the toast was burnt?

MAN: Yes. Although I couldn't see the color, I think the toast was very burnt. It had the taste of coal. You might say it was pure coal.

DOCTOR: Very good, I understand now. First we find the cause of the problem, then the treatment.

MAN: I hope this medicine doesn't taste too bad. My stomach hurts so much.

DOCTOR: This is not something you drink. My assistant just prepared a bottle of eye medicine.

MAN: Eye medicine for the stomach? How does it work?

DOCTOR: This medicine illuminates the eyes and increases their power of sight. Lean back sir so I can put these drops into your eyes.

MAN: Doctor, are you making fun of me? Stop fooling around! What are you doing?

DOCTOR: I'm trying to help you. Now, lean back.

MAN: I come to you with a stomach problem, and you want to put medicine in my eyes. What connection is there between my stomach and my eyes?

DOCTOR: Sir, you yourself have just told me that you ate burnt toast that was like coal instead of good bread, and you didn't see the color.

MAN: Yes, that's right.

DOCTOR: I want to first treat your eyes so that you won't eat burnt toast in place of good toast in the future; then you won't have stomach problems.

MAN: How can you be sure?

DOCTOR: For a person who can taste the difference between toast and coal, but can't see the difference, treating his eyes takes priority over treating his stomach!

The End

The Duck's Mistake

<u>Cast</u>
YOUNG DUCK
NARRATOR 1
NARRATOR 2
OLD DUCK

NARRATOR 1: Once there was a young duck that lived in a garden.

NARRATOR 2: There was a small lake in the garden that contained a lot of fish. The duck had heard that the fish tasted good, but it hadn't seen any.

NARRATOR 1: One moonlit night, the duck went to the lake to try and catch some fish. Peering into the lake, the duck saw the reflection of the moon.

YOUNG DUCK: What is that big white thing? Is that a fish? I'm going to jump on it!

NARRATOR 2: It jumped on the reflection, but it couldn't find anything. When the duck got out of the water, the waves it had made broke up the image of the moon, so the duck thought the fish had fled away.

NARRATOR 1: But after a while, the water became smooth again, and the reflection of the moon was visible again.

YOUNG DUCK: There is that big, white fish. I will jump, attack, and eat it!

NARRATOR 2: Once again, the duck jumped on the reflection of the moon in the water and found nothing. Exhausted, the duck gave up looking for fish that night.

YOUNG DUCK: Catching fish is hard work!

NARRATOR 1: The next night, the duck wanted to taste fish again.

YOUNG DUCK: I'm hungry! I want fish for dinner!

NARRATOR 2: The duck went to the lake, and, again, it saw the reflection of the moon on the water.

NARRATOR 1: The duck repeated his mistake from the night before. Despite his efforts, the duck went home empty-handed.

YOUNG DUCK: This is very unhappy and frustrating work. Why can't I catch that big white fish?

NARRATOR 2: The next day, the young duck asked an old duck about how to catch fish at night.

YOUNG DUCK: I have heard that fish taste very good, and I have tried to catch one. But it can't be done.

OLD DUCK: Why not? How did you try to catch the fish?

YOUNG DUCK: I saw something round and bright in the water, and as soon as I tried to grab it, it disappeared. After a while, it reappeared. I tried to grab it, and it got away again.

OLD DUCK: Fool! That wasn't a fish at all, but the reflection of the moon in the sky on the water. You were trying to catch a reflection instead of a fish.

YOUNG DUCK: That big white, round thing wasn't a fish?

OLD DUCK: Of course not. Now, don't tell anyone about this or they will laugh at you. Don't try to catch the moon any more. One lesson is enough. No repeats.

YOUNG DUCK: You're right. I made a mistake.

NARRATOR 1: The young duck was so embarrassed that it did not have the courage to ask the old duck about fish and what fish looked like.

NARRATOR 2: The young duck didn't realize that there is no shame in asking and learning. If it had asked what fish look like, then the old duck would have told it.

NARRATOR 1: On the following nights, whenever the duck saw fish in the water, it thought that the fish were also the reflection of the moon.

YOUNG DUCK: Anyone who tries something a second time will regret it.

NARRATOR 2: So the duck gave up trying to catch fish and never tasted one.

NARRATOR 1: This was the story of the bashful duck that was discouraged by one mistake and abandoned its goal.

NARRATOR2: It called its mistake "experience" and thus lost all.

The End

The Nightingale's Quick Wit

<u>Cast</u>
NARRATOR
MR. LIVELY
NIGHTINGALE

NARRATOR: Once there was a gardener with good taste who had a fine green garden. There were many different kinds of beautiful and fragrant flowers growing there. Every morning when the sun rose, the gardener would go into the garden and walk on the grass and among the flowers. Since he was so cheerful, his friends called him Old Mr. Lively.

MR. LIVELY: The heart of a person who spends a few minutes walking in clean fresh morning air through flowers and trees will never grow old.

NARRATOR: Amongst all the many flowers planted in his garden, Mr. Lively had a favorite rosebush.

MR. LIVELY: This rosebush has the most beautiful and most fragrant flowers out of all of the flowers in my garden.

NARRATOR: Mr. Lively loved to smell each of his favorite flowers early in the morning.

MR. LIVELY: The nightingales are right to love flowers so much. Grass and flowers are the delight of life and the source of energy.

NARRATOR: One morning when the sun had not yet risen above the horizon and the light was dim, the gardener went to walk in the garden as usual. When he came to the rose bush, he saw a nightingale sitting on one of the branches, its beak buried in the heart of the flower, nosing its bright red petals this way and that. The bird was singing happily. As a result of the bird burying its beak in the petals, the rose fell apart, and all the petals fell to the ground.

MR. LIVELY: I love to hear the song of the nightingale, and it is charming to see the bird on my favorite rosebush, but I don't like the fact that it destroyed the flower.

NARRATOR: After several minutes, the bird noticed the presence of the gardener and flew off. The next morning, the gardener saw the nightingale behaving with the rose as it had done the day before. It was singing with its head in the blossom. When the bird spied the gardener, it flew away.

MR. LIVELY: That bird is destroying my favorite flowers, one by one! The nightingale has a right to love the flowers, but a flower is to be seen and smelled, not torn apart and destroyed. This won't do. I work hard to cultivate these flowers, and the nightingale keeps coming to tear them apart.

NARRATOR: The following morning, Mr. Lively again saw the nightingale busy in conversation with another flower, and its petals were falling to the ground.

MR. LIVELY: *(Angry.)* When a nightingale misuses its freedom, it should be put in a cage!

NARRATOR: So that day, he set traps and nets among the roses, and the next morning he caught the bird and imprisoned it in a cage.

MR. LIVELY: You didn't know the value of freedom. Now stay here until you learn what tearing roses apart means!

NIGHTINGALE: Dear friend, we are both lovers of flowers, are we not?

MR. LIVELY: Yes, but I grow them and take care of them, and you destroy them!

NIGHTINGALE: Er, by taking care of the flowers, you are the reason for my delight. I sing to the flowers, and you enjoy my singing.

MR. LIVELY: You do have a beautiful voice.

NIGHTINGALE: Why have you put me in this prison? I want to move about the garden as freely as you do. If you have put me in a cage to hear my singing, then know that my nest is in your garden, and I shall sing for you day and night.

MR. LIVELY: No, this isn't about the singing.

NIGHTINGALE: Is there some other reason you have put me in a cage?

MR. LIVELY: Yes, there is a good reason.

NIGHTINGALE: Tell me what it is!

MR. LIVELY: You have caused me a lot of misery and injured several of my dear flowers. When you should control yourself, you lose control and disturb the flowers so much their petals fall. You deserve to stay put in a cage and be prohibited from entering the garden. This is the punishment that your behavior has earned for you. Let it serve as an example to others!

NIGHTINGALE: Unjust man! By throwing me into this prison, you have deprived me of the pleasure of moving about your garden, and you have broken my heart. You have made me miserable. And then you talk about punishment! Don't you think that if punishment is to be handed out, you are more deserving of it than I? I destroy flowers, but you destroy hearts!

MR. LIVELY: I hadn't thought about it that way.

NARRATOR: The nightingale's words affected the gardener. He opened the door of the cage and freed the bird. The nightingale flew to the rosebush and sat on one of the branches.

NIGHTINGALE: You have done right by me; I shall do right by you. Know that beneath the very ground upon which you stand, there is hidden a pot filled with gold coins. Take it and enjoy it.

NARRATOR: The man dug up the ground and saw that the nightingale had spoken the truth.

MR. LIVELY: I am amazed that you can spot a pot of gold under the ground, but how is it you didn't spot the nets I had set out?

NIGHTINGALE: There are two reasons. The first is that no matter how wise and sharp-sighted a person may be, there is also sometimes the matter of fate, accident, and misfortune, and a person is caught.

MR. LIVELY: What is the second reason?

NIGHTINGALE: The second is that because I am not interested in gold, I see it and pass it by. But I love flowers and am mad about them. I abandon the evidence of my eyes, ears, and brain when I am among them. Thus, I fell into your trap among the flowers. Too much of anything, even love, may be the source of much sorrow and pain.

NARRATOR: Having said this, the nightingale flew off to find another flower to love.

The End

The Sin of the Hen

Cast
NARRATOR
FALCON
HEN

NARRATOR: Once there was a hunting falcon that had been injured in flight by an arrow. It was no longer able to fly, and it managed to glide to the earth, crying in pain. It landed near a hen that was busy eating grain on the ground.

HEN: Oh poor falcon. Are you hurt badly? I hope it is not serious. If there is anything I can do for you, please tell me.

FALCON: Even if there is something you can do, I don't want you to do it.

HEN: Why not?

FALCON: Get away from me! We can never get along with each other. I don't care for your behavior.

HEN: Please don't be unkind. What have I done that seeing me displeases you so?

FALCON: You are ungrateful. You have no idea of loyalty and generosity. I am a generous and noble bird, and it would be shameful for me to know disloyal birds.

HEN: *(Astonished.)* Why do you spout these accusations at me? Have I been disloyal to you in some way that you have such a bad opinion of me? I am a hen, and you are a falcon. A noble bird is one whose words have a reasonable basis. Why do you say I am disloyal?

FALCON: The sign of your disloyalty is this: People treat you very well. They give you water and food. They give you a place and a home. They spend their days and nights taking care of you. It is through their kindness that you have what you have.

HEN: The farmer does give me grain, and he built the chicken coop.

FALCON: Despite all this, whenever they want to catch you, you run away from them! You run into this corner and out of that one. You show no gratitude, and you are afraid of your masters.

HEN: But you were born a wild falcon. Aren't you afraid of your masters?

FALCON: After we become acquainted with someone for a few days and come to like him and eat the food he gives us, we are unflinchingly loyal. We hunt for him. Whenever we are far from him, as soon as he whistles to us, we return directly and sit on his arm or shoulder. We don't run away, and we are more familiar with him than you chickens.

HEN: Since you are using proofs in your speech, I shall answer your proofs.

FALCON: I'm glad to see that even though you aren't loyal, at least you are reasonable.

HEN: The reason people sometimes think that others are guilty and have a bad opinion of them is because they don't know what is in each other's hearts. They look at the outside and judge from one point of view.

FALCON: Is that so?

HEN: Yes, and you are making the same mistake about me. You see me running away, but you know nothing of my sorrows.

FALCON: What sorrows can a well-kept hen possibly have?

HEN: In return for the food they give you, you hunt for them. In return for the food they give me, I give them my eggs.

FALCON: In this point we are the same.

HEN: It is not the same; I must give them my children.

FALCON: People expect some kind of payment for the food they give you. There is no such thing as a free lunch. Can you hunt?

HEN: No.

FALCON: Then the price is your eggs.

HEN: But it is more than just the eggs. The reason for your returning and my fleeing is that you have never seen a falcon roasting on a spit and do not fear for your life! I've seen many chickens roasting on a spit and served on plates! I fear for my own life.

FALCON: I've never seen a falcon roasting over a fire.

HEN: If you had, you would never get near a human being again. If I jump from roof to roof to escape, you would flee from mountain to mountain. Am I right?

FALCON: Yes. I was just looking at the appearance of what you do.

HEN: Do you understand that you shouldn't judge things by appearances?

FALCON: Yes. Many things may appear wrong, but in truth, if we knew the reason, we would forgive them and admit that they are not at fault.

HEN: So now can I help you with your injury?

FALCON: Yes.

NARRATOR: The two birds became friends, and the falcon quickly recovered from his injury.

The End

The World-Traveling Pigeon

<u>Cast</u>
NARRATOR
PLAYER, a pigeon
MUSICIAN, a pigeon
FALCON
EAGLE
TRAITOR PIGEON

NARRATOR: There once lived two pigeons that were good friends. They told each other stories, sang together, and during the day they searched the countryside for tasty seeds and grains. They enjoyed life. One of them was named Player, and one was named Musician. One day when they were flying about playfully in the fields, Player pointed out a distant mountain covered with greenery to Musician.

PLAYER: I wonder what that place is like. Let's go and see it.

MUSICIAN: No, brother. It's a long way off. I don't think it's a good idea to try and to go that far away. Anyway, it can't be any more pleasant that this place where we are right now! Besides, there might be a hunter, an enemy, or some other danger there.

PLAYER: Danger? Poof! You're acting like a scared chicken! It seems you don't know that I have decided to visit the ends of the earth and learn about everything.

MUSICIAN: When did you decide this?

PLAYER: To tell you the truth, this life we have here is boring and dull. This isn't life!

MUSICIAN: What are you talking about?

PLAYER: Every night we sleep in a nest we call home, and every day we roam about this wilderness we call our homeland.

I'm tired of it. The world is big, and one should be a world traveler.

MUSICIAN: Dear friend, the world is the same wherever you go. As the poet said, "Wherever you travel, the sky is the same color." If a person is wise, he can live anywhere and be happy there! Travel is tiring and dangerous. Here we have a good place to live, peace, and food. We are free and secure. We have a thousand friends and acquaintances. Why should we go somewhere else and be strangers and homeless? Beyond our homeland, no one will respect us or play with us.

PLAYER: I completely disagree. I've heard that travel is very beneficial. You gain experience by going to foreign lands. Wise men have said, "Until the pen travels on the paper, nothing is accomplished," and "Until the sword leaves the scabbard when on the battlefield, honor is not won." And, "Water which stands in one place becomes stagnant." All the great men of history have praised travel and seeing the world. If this place where we live now were really so good, why don't hawks, eagles, and peacocks come and live here?

MUSICIAN: What an odd thing to say! What have pens and swords to do with us? Everyone has a life that is suited to him. Travel is good for falconers and horsemen, but not for pigeons and chickens. Haven't the wise also said that when a fish is taken out of water, it dies; or, that many people have perished at the hands of enemies and bandits?

PLAYER: Well, maybe I've heard a few of those stories. I don't remember.

MUSICIAN: If you don't know, then I'll tell you. There are many others who envy us for our happy lives. If a person doesn't know the value of what he has and becomes a beggar in a foreign country, following strangers, then he will surely regret it! I know how sweet it is to be with one's friends. Separation from friends and one's kith and kin is the worst of pains and the greatest of sorrows.

PLAYER: Your words mean nothing to me! The world is a big place, and there will be no shortage of friends and acquaintances. If today I am separated from one, tomorrow I'll find another. I'm not afraid of the hardships of travel. Why? Because one gets used to it. Seeing the world is worth the pain of being a stranger.

MUSICIAN: Don't make such a serious mistake. Life is short. If you flit about trying to find a new friend and a new place every day, as soon as you get to know him and that place, you'll be off again. You will waste your life testing things superficially and not taking the time to know someone or some place really well. The best friends are old friends, and the best life is that of your homeland.

PLAYER: Please don't bore me with your philosophy! I've made up my mind, and I won't change it. I think seeing the world is better than eating it. I'm going to set out right this minute. Don't people live in other places? I'll be one of them!

MUSICIAN: Since you won't listen to my advice, it is clear that you are one of those birds that won't learn anything without hitting your head against a rock. Do what you will! But if you are mistreated by others, I am still faithful to our friendship. Whenever you regret your choice and return, I'll welcome you back.

NARRATOR: So they said farewell to each other. Musician returned to his nest while Player excitedly flew off, its wings beating, towards the green mountain shimmering in the distance. The bird flew on and on until it reached a planted field on the slopes of the mountain. In that place there were trees, flowers, and grasslands. The climate was mild and pleasant. Since the sun was low in the sky, the bird decided to stay the night there. It flew to the limb of a tall tree and sat down.

PLAYER: How wonderful it is to live on a limb high in a tree, to have a view of the plants and the stream, and to see the sparkling stars in the dark sky at night.

NARRATOR: As soon as the sun had set, the weather changed suddenly. The soft wind began to blow hard, and a terrible storm started. Thunder rolled, and lightning flashed. Rain poured down heavily. There was no place in the tree for Player to take shelter from the rain and cold. So, it crouched under the limbs and leaves until morning, shivering from the cold and wet.

PLAYER: What have I done to come to this unknown place? Why did I ignore the words of my faithful friend? The weather won't always be like this. It will pass. If I am disheartened by a little bad luck, I'll never get anywhere. I must be strong and patient.

NARRATOR: The day dawned, the storm had indeed passed, and the sun was shining brightly. The mountain glowed in the beauty of the clear day, and the pigeon flew up to a branch and admired the view. However, since it didn't know the other birds that were flying about and it didn't understand their language, it felt a little lonely. As much as it tried to sing, it wasn't able to.

PLAYER: Maybe I should go home. No, I've taken the decision to spend some days in traveling about the world.

NARRATOR: While the pigeon was considering both sides of this issue, it spied a strong-taloned falcon flying toward it, intent upon snatching it away! Player's heart pounded rapidly at the sight of its enemy.

PLAYER: Look at that falcon! Look at his huge claws! He's coming right at me!

FALCON: Hello, breakfast! Now hold still so I can catch you.

NARRATOR: Player hadn't recovered yet from the cold and misery of the night, and now this!

PLAYER: Oh Musician, you were right! If I escape this evil falcon, I will forget about world travel and return to you, my faithful friend.

NARRATOR: As Player was praying and swearing to return to its friend, it saw an eagle with sharp talons extended swooping toward it from another direction! Now it had two enemies. Player trembled in terror, not knowing what to do. The eagle was circling the tree in which Player had taken shelter.

EAGLE: Is this little pigeon worthy of being my breakfast? Yes, I think this pigeon is worthy of being the breakfast of an eagle!

NARRATOR: As the eagle dived at the pigeon, talons ready to grab the small bird, at that very moment, the falcon swooped down, trying to get to Player before the eagle.

EAGLE: Hey, you falcon! I am the king of birds, and this pigeon is mine. If you get a foot closer, I'll skin your head!

FALCON: Don't upset yourself for nothing. The pigeon is mine because I saw it first.

NARRATOR: The two birds of prey began to fight each other, talons slashing, feathers flying.

PLAYER: When enemies fight each other, it is the time of freedom for friends.

NARRATOR: Player dropped from the high branch and flew into a little hole under a stone on the ground. It was suffocating from the tightness of the space, but it didn't dare leave the hole out of fear of the falcon and the eagle. He stayed there all day and all night.

PLAYER: I'm miserable in this hole. I'm hungry. I miss my friend, Musician.

NARRATOR: With the coming of the morning and bright sunshine, Player became more confident.

PLAYER: I don't hear any fighting out there. Maybe it is safe to come out?

NARRATOR: Slowly and carefully, the pigeon came out of the hole and flew off to search for something to eat. As it was flying about, it saw a plump pigeon sitting on the ground surrounded by grains of rice and millet.

PLAYER: I'm starving! And now I have found something to eat!

NARRATOR: Player landed near the plump pigeon, and thinking only of its hunger, it began to select the grains and seeds it wanted to eat.

PLAYER: Let's see, what should I start with? Rice or millet?

NARRATOR: But after the first bite, it realized that it had fallen into a trap, and its feet were tangled in a net.

PLAYER: Hey! What is this? My feet are stuck.

NARRATOR: Player was trapped in the net.

PLAYER: You there, plump pigeon, we are the same kind of bird. When I saw you here, I was deceived and fell into this net. You should have warned me so that I wouldn't fall into it.

TRAITOR PIGEON: You think that is my job?

PLAYER: I am your guest. Why didn't you tell the truth?

TRAITOR PIGEON: There are four reasons for my silence.

PLAYER: I'm listening. Out with it, what is the first reason?

TRAITOR PIGEON: First, it is true we are the same kind, but I make my living this way. The hunter keeps me and feeds me every day and then places me in the trap to lure other birds such as yourself into this trap. If I do not do this for him, he would make minced kabob out of me.

PLAYER: I can hardly believe it. You work for the hunter. What a strange place this is. What is your second reason?

TRAITOR PIGEON: You have two eyes in your head to open and see the paths and pitfalls of life. As soon as you saw the food, you should have thought about a trap. If you had been smart, you would have realized that there are no rice fields in this region, and no one gives rice away for nothing! No one scatters rice for your honor for nothing else.

PLAYER: Well, you never know ... I mean maybe. Oh, you're right. I should have been more careful. I was just really hungry after spending the night in a hole. What is your third reason?

TRAITOR PIGEON: I was feeling lonely, and there was no one to share my misfortune. I hoped that you would fall into the trap so that I would have a companion for at least a little while.

PLAYER: You were lonely?

TRAITOR PIGEON: Don't you realize that birds that have been misled and are helpless want the same thing to happen to others? Then other birds will not blame them for their carelessness.

PLAYER: What is your fourth reason?

TRAITOR PIGEON: I did not invite you to eat the food and be my guest. It's your own fault that you hurried and did not ask me whose food this was. Now you must stay here until you come to your senses and consider your situation. Don't think just about filling your stomach all the time!

PLAYER: All right. I am grateful for your wisdom. Now, in the way of kindness and graciousness, can you show me any way to escape from the net so that I may employ your counsel in my life?

TRAITOR PIGEON: You are a big fool. If I knew a way of escape, don't you think I would have used it myself?

PLAYER: You don't like working for the hunter?

TRAITOR PIGEON: Of course not. But our fate is sealed. It is our destiny, and there is no remedy. Your situation is just like that of the baby camel that said to his mother in the caravan, "Dear Mother, I'm exhausted from all this walking. Let's stop and rest a while." His mother replied, "If it were up to me, I would not be carrying this burden either, but somebody else is holding the reins."

PLAYER: You'll never help me. You are convinced of your own helplessness. With all these calamities, I must not lose heart. I must do something, and I must not blame my misfortune or good fortune on destiny. For every problem, there is a solution.

NARRATOR: Player the Pigeon thought for a while, and then he attacked the cords of the net with his beak and tore them apart. With a sudden burst of energy, he was able to free his feet, take wing, and fly away. It was his good fortune that some of the cords of the net were rotten.

PLAYER: If I had not exerted myself, I would still be in that net!

NARRATOR: With much effort, Player flew towards his homeland. It flew on and on until it came to a field where it landed to eat some food. The bird sat on the wall of a ruin.

PLAYER: This is cultivated land, and a village is nearby. I don't have to worry about birds of prey.

NARRATOR: At that moment, a boy happened to be passing by the wall. He spotted the pigeon on the mud brick wall. Taking out his slingshot, he aimed at the pigeon. The stone shot up and hit Player in the side. The bird fell off the wall and right into a well that was at the foot of the wall. The village boy saw that he couldn't get the pigeon out of the well, so he walked away.

PLAYER: At least I am safe for the moment in this well. My side hurts. All this is my own fault. I didn't listen to the advice of my friend, and I set out by myself to unknown parts without any planning. Anyone who wants to travel must first learn about the places he wants to visit and about the ways of life there. So far I have found a way out of every misfortune that my recklessness has brought upon me.

NARRATOR: The next day, Player felt better, though the bird was still weak. With a lot of trouble, it managed to get up to the top of the well. It immediately set off straight for home.

MUSICIAN: What is that sound I hear? Could it be the wings of my dear friend Player? Player, is that you?

PLAYER: Yes, it is me. More dead than alive, but I made it back home.

MUSICIAN: You are tired, and you are hurt! What happened to you?

PLAYER: I heard that traveling the world had many benefits and experiences. I thought that other parts of the world were better than ours. Now I have learned that though the world has many places worth seeing, our happiness and peace is in the seeing of our families and our friends who have the same heart and tongue as we do. So it is that after a trip into the outside world, we learn the value of our homeland and the goodness of our own friends.

The End

Cooperation

Cast
CROW
TAQWI, a Pigeon leader
PIGEON 1
PIGEON 2
ZIRAK, a mouse
DEER
TURTLE
HUNTER
NARRATOR

NARRATOR: One day, while flying about, a black crow came upon a beautiful region and decided to land on a tree and look about at the scenery. It saw a hunter approaching, and at first the crow was frightened, imagining the hunter might be looking for it.

CROW: No, as long as there are pigeons, deer, rabbits, and other animals around, no one would want to shoot a crow. Danger is for those who have some value or use. Let's see where this hunter is going and what he's up to.

NARRATOR: The hunter didn't bother to look up at the crow. At a little distance from the tree in which the crow was perched, he spread his net and scattered some seed and grain as bait.

HUNTER: I'll catch some nice plump birds for my dinner. Now all I have to do is wait.

NARRATOR: The hunter walked away to the shade of a tree and lay down to take a nap.

CROW: That hunter was right about just having to wait; here come some chubby pigeons.

NARRATOR: As soon as the birds spied the seeds, they wanted to land on the ground and eat.

PIGEON 1: Look at all that millet seed. Time for lunch!

PIGEON 2: I call the barley seed. It looks delicious! Let's eat.

TAQWI: Wait, my friends! Don't be in a hurry.

PIGEON 1: What is it, Taqwi?

TAQWI: Let's make sure there is no danger.

PIGEON 1: Danger? Here? I don't think so.

PIGEON 2: No time. We're very hungry, and someone may come and eat the food before we do.

PIGEON 1: What danger can there possibly be in the middle of the wilderness?

NARRATOR: The pigeons landed and were caught in the net.

PIGEON 1 and PIGEON 2: Help! Help! We're caught in the net!

TAQWI: Shh. There is a hunter under the tree sleeping. Be quiet!

PIGEON 1: But what are we going to do? We are stuck in this net.

PIGEON 2: I'm scared.

TAQWI: Listen, friends, you were hasty. Capture is the result and outcome of your haste and thoughtlessness.

PIGEON 1: We don't have time for a lecture. We have to get away before the hunter wakes up.

PIGEON 2: If we waste time, we'll never free ourselves.

TAQWI: If each one of us is only thinking of himself, we are lost. We must unite and work together. If we cooperate with each other, we will be saved.

PIGEON 1 and PIGEON 2: What should we do? Tell us what to do!

TAQWI: If we work together, we can all fly up in the sky at once. We will lift the net and carry it with us.

PIGEON 1: How are we going to get out of the net?

TAQWI: I'll explain that later.

PIGEON 2: Oh no, the hunter is waking up! He is coming over here!

HUNTER: Looks like I'll be having roast pigeon for dinner tonight!

TAQWI: On the count of three, we all beat our wings together! 1… 2 … 3!

NARRATOR: They beat their wings and slowly they pulled the net off the ground and rose into the air. At Taqwi's direction, they flew ahead. The hunter ran after them.

HUNTER: Those are some clever birds, but they will get tired soon enough; then I will catch them.

NARRATOR: When the hunter ran faster, the pigeons flew faster. The crow watched this scene with great interest for it had never seen such a sight in its lifetime.

CROW: Who would have thought those silly birds could organize themselves so well? That Taqwi can keep his head under stress. I'm going to follow them and see what happens next.

NARRATOR: The chase continued with the pigeons flying in the sky ahead of the pursuing hunter.

TAQWI: Friends, the hunter will never stop chasing us as long as he can see us.

PIGEON 1: I don't think I can go on for much longer at this pace.

PIGEON 2: You have to go on, or we will fall to the ground, and the hunter will catch us!

TAQWI: Let's change direction and go behind some walls so that he won't be able to see us. He'll give up the chase then.

NARRATOR: The pigeons in the net changed direction, headed toward a village, and hid behind the walls.

HUNTER: I'll never catch them now. They'll land in someone's yard, and that person will claim my pigeons — and my net! I give up.

NARRATOR: The hunter headed back into the woods to set another trap.

PIGEON 1: We lost that hunter, but now what do we do?

PIGEON 2: How are we going to get out of this net?

TAQWI: We can't do it ourselves. We need the help and cooperation of others.

PIGEON 1: Who do you have in mind?

TAQWI: I know a mouse that I've helped in the past. The mouse's name is Zirak.

PIGEON 2: How is a mouse going to help us?

TAQWI: He can cut the cords of the net with his teeth.

PIGEON 1: He would help us?

TAQWI: It is in this kind of situation that the faithfulness of friendship and kindness is made apparent.

NARRATOR: They landed on a ruin where the mouse had his home.

TAQWI: Zirak! Zirak, come out! It is I, Taqwi, and I need your help.

ZIRAK: Squeak. Taqwi, how nice of you to visit, and you've brought friends. Um, what's that on your feet?

TAQWI: We got stuck in the hunter's net.

ZIRAK: Kind friend, with all your knowledge and experience, how did you come to fall into the net?

PIGEON 2: That was our fault.

PIGEON 1: We were greedy for food.

PIGEON 2: We were also too hasty and didn't look carefully.

TAQWI: Sometimes pigeons make mistakes, but the intelligent one does not surrender to these things and lose hope.

PIGEON 1: This is not the time for talk. We need to act quickly in case that hunter is still around.

TAQWI: Can you save us from this net by cutting the cords with your teeth?

ZIRAK: Yes, that should be possible, but it might take some time. These cords are tough.

NARRATOR: Zirak the mouse began to free Taqwi first.

TAQWI: Dear friend Zirak, please cut my friends free first.

ZIRAK: I'll get to them. Don't you love your own life? You have done many good things for me, and I want to free you first.

TAQWI: Thank you for your loyalty, but I know that since you are my friend, you will not neglect to free me no matter how tired you may be. But if you free me first, I fear that when you get tired, you may leave the others trapped in the net.

ZIRAK: But weren't they the ones that got you stuck in this net in the first place?

TAQWI: Yes, but without their help, I could not have escaped from the hunter. In times of calamity and hardship, a leader must share the sorrow of his followers and remain with them as he would in times of happiness and rejoicing. For these reasons, I beg you to free my companions first.

ZIRAK: What shining words. Indeed the signs of leadership and greatness are sympathy and feeling for one's people.

NARRATOR: The mouse cut the cords and strings of the net and freed all the pigeons.

PIGEON 1: Thank you, Zirak!

PIGEON 2: You have saved us!

TAQWI: I will not forget your kindness, my friend! Farewell until we meet again.

ZIRAK: Stay out of trouble, and I hope to see you again in happier circumstances! Good-bye! Squeak.

NARRATOR: The mouse went back into his home. The crow, who had watched Zirak's unselfish aid of the pigeons, applauded the mouse for its actions.

CROW: This mouse is special. I would like to be its friend. Most crows eat mice, but if we are friends, I won't eat Zirak. No one is immune from misfortune, and to have such a sincere friend would indeed be a blessing.

NARRATOR: The crow went to the mouse's home and called to him.

CROW: Caaa! Zirak! Zirak! Caa! Caaa!

ZIRAK: Squeak. I don't know you. How do you know my name? What do you want?

CROW: I'm a crow. I live in a meadow near a creek. Until this day, I was your enemy, but I happened to be passing by today. I saw the entanglement of the pigeons and witnessed your generosity and loyalty.

ZIRAK: Taqwi is my friend. One must help friends in times of hardship and celebrate with them in times of happiness.

CROW: Now I understand the value of friendship and cooperation. I have the great desire and hope that you will accept me as your friend and helper. After this, I shall be faithful to your friendship with all my heart and soul.

ZIRAK: Thank you for your kind words, but you must know that there can be no friendship between us.

CROW: Why not?

ZIRAK: Because mice are the food of crows, and the crows are our enemies.

CROW: I am aware of this. But when I know the value of your friendship, I can't possibly harm you.

ZIRAK: Friendship has no meaning between the strong and the weak, or between a sheep and a butcher. People can truly become friends who benefit and do not harm each other. That is the first rule of friendship.

CROW: I completely agree with this rule.

ZIRAK: That's good, but a true friend is also the well-wisher of his friend's friends. A wise person must avoid the friend of his enemies as well as the enemy of his friends. As long as you retain your friendship with other crows and oppress other mice, what would your friendship with me mean?

CROW: Zirak, I am so pleased with your generosity and loyalty that I won't be friends with other crows. I won't harm any more mice. I am not one who deceives others with a thousand oaths and promises and then later takes advantage of them. I am nothing more than a black crow, but to the extent of my crowhood, I am honorable!

NARRATOR: They talked much more and told each other many stories. Finally, the mouse was convinced that the crow was really speaking the truth. They swore the oath of friendship and unity. Zirak came out of the shelter of his home, and the two new friends delighted in the sight of each other. For several days, they exchanged stories of faithfulness and betrayal among various kinds of animals.

ZIRAK: I think it would be a good idea if you were to build a nest right here so that we can be near each other.

CROW: Well, in this place, there is a considerable traffic of hunters and travelers. It's not very quiet and secure.

ZIRAK: Do you know of a better place?

CROW: I do. In the fields near a creek there is a turtle that is my friend. This area is very pleasant, and there is plenty of food for you and for me. Why don't you move near Turtle and me? I'm sure we'd enjoy ourselves more.

ZIRAK: This sounds like a good suggestion. I'd like to meet Turtle. Let's go at once.

NARRATOR: The crow put the mouse in a small basket. Taking the handle in its beak, it flew to the creek where Turtle lived. The turtle first hid itself in the water.

CROW: Turtle, Turtle, where are you? I want you to meet my friend Zirak the mouse.

TURTLE: Blub blub. *(Clears throat.)* Ahem. It's you, Crow. You have been gone for a while, but I am so glad you are here now. Is this a new friend?

ZIRAK: Squeak. I am Zirak. It is a pleasure to meet you, Turtle.

TURTLE: What nice manners you have, Zirak.

NARRATOR: Crow told the turtle all about Zirak freeing the pigeons. The turtle had also seen much of the world and was very wise. It praised the mouse for helping the pigeons, and the three fell to talking.

ZIRAK: What's that sound?

TURTLE: It is a deer; it is running straight toward us! Hide!

NARRATOR: Thinking that a hunter must be after it, the crow flew up the tree, the mouse ran into a hole, and the turtle dove into the water. But when the deer reached the creek, it stopped and drank some water. Then it raised its head, stood motionless, and looked at the fields around it.

CROW: Hey, there isn't any hunter chasing that deer. Turtle, Zirak, come out of your hiding places.

TURTLE: Blub blub. *(Clears throat.)* Ahem. So, Miss Deer, why are you so anxious? There is no hunter chasing you. Where did you come from?

DEER: *(Giggles.)* I live alone in this region. For some time, I have lived peacefully, grazing on the grass as I wished. Today I saw something dark in the distance. I thought that it was an enemy, so I fled here. If I'm bothering you, please forgive me. I don't want to cause you any trouble.

TURTLE: You are a harmless animal. This is a secure, comfortable place. We are three well-matched friends who wish to live here in peace. If you want to, you may become our friend and join us.

DEER: Why yes, I would like that very much.

NARRATOR: So the deer stayed there. Everyday the animals met together and chatted. The old turtle was the best storyteller, and they all were happy and enjoyed each other's company. But one day, when the crow, the mouse, and the turtle met in their usual place at the usual time, the deer did not show up. They became worried.

ZIRAK: Friend Crow, could you please fly around and see where Miss Deer is at the moment?

CROW: Yes, I'll go at once. This is very unlike her to miss our story time.

NARRATOR: The crow flapped its wings and took off, soaring in spirals around the countryside. It returned quickly with news.

CROW: Alas, my friends. I have found our friend Deer, but she is in a bad situation.

TURTLE: What is the problem?

CROW: She is trapped in a hunter's net near a weeping willow tree.

TURTLE: Zirak, it is time for your help. Hurry to the deer, and free her from the net.

NARRATOR: The crow took the mouse by the tail and flew to the deer. Zirak began to cut the cords of the net with his sharp teeth. When it had finally freed the deer, the turtle had managed to come upon the scene to express its sorrow at the deer's plight.

DEER: Friend Turtle, we have always benefited from your experience. Now is the time to flee. Why did you, who have such slow feet, come here?

TURTLE: I was acting out of friendship. I came to share your misfortune.

CROW: Now it is time to go home quickly!

ZIRAK: Yes, move faster, Turtle.

NARRATOR: As soon as the turtle was moving, the crow flew off, and the deer and mouse ran as fast as they could. At that moment, the hunter came to his net and found the strings and cords cut.

HUNTER: What's this? Was there a deer in here? How did it cut through my net?

NARRATOR: The hunter looked around, picked up the net with a sigh, and was starting to go home when he saw the turtle moving slowly away.

HUNTER: Though a turtle isn't anything special, it is better than nothing.

NARRATOR: The hunter picked up the turtle, put it in a sack, and tied the opening shut with a stout cord.

TURTLE: Help! Help me!

NARRATOR: The hunter threw the sack over his shoulder.

TURTLE: Umph.

HUNTER: Time to go home, turtle. Turtle soup for dinner. *(Laughs.)*

TURTLE: Oh no! Help!

NARRATOR: When the crow, the mouse, and the deer met again, they looked for the turtle. When they couldn't find their friend, they realized that the hunter had carried it off. The deer was very upset at this turn of events.

DEER: Whaaah! It's my mistake that has caused all of this trouble. Turtle came to comfort me, and now it has been captured by the hunter. Whaah! Now there isn't anything we can do. *(Starts sobbing.)*

CROW: Deer, stop crying. Why can't we do something? As long as a group of friends is united and work together and are willing to sacrifice and cooperate, anything can be done. We can save our friend.

DEER: Tell us what to do.

ZIRAK: Do you have a plan, Crow?

CROW: Everyone pay attention. We want to put on a good little play. Friend Deer, you will run and lie down by the path the hunter is taking.

DEER: Lie down in the middle of the path?

CROW: Yes, like you are resting. Then I will come and attack you as though I wanted to pluck out your eyes. That will attract the attention of the hunter.

DEER: You're not really going to scratch my eyes, are you?

CROW: Of course not; it's an act. After I pretend to attack you, you must get up as though you're afraid of me and very, very slowly, you'll limp off.

DEER: What is the point of limping?

CROW: When the hunter sees that you can't run, he'll want to catch you. When he gets near you, you'll go a little faster. The hunter will try to keep up with you.

ZIRAK: What is the point of this chase?

CROW: The hunter will eventually have to put his sack down on the ground to catch the deer. Then you, friend mouse, will arrive at the sack and cut it open with your teeth.

ZIRAK: Then turtle will come out!

CROW: Yes, he must hide himself while the rest of us will get away as fast as we can.

DEER and ZIRAK: Great plan, Crow! Let's do it!

NARRATOR: The deer ran into the field and lay down by the path that the hunter was taking. The crow attacked the deer. The deer got up and limped slowly off. The hunter followed the deer, trying to catch it. The deer increased its speed, and the hunter was forced to put his sack down in order to run faster. The mouse immediately started to cut the sack open. The deer stopped running and lay down in order to keep the hunter after it. Whenever the hunter got near, the deer would scramble to its feet and trot off. Meanwhile, the crow was flying about keeping an eye on the progress of the mouse working on the sack. As soon as the turtle was freed and had hidden itself, the crow signaled the deer. The deer immediately galloped off at top speed.

HUNTER: Well, that's it. I'm never going to catch that deer. I'd better go back and get my sack with the juicy turtle.

NARRATOR: When the hunter found the sack, he was astounded to see it cut open.

HUNTER: What's this? My sack cut open? Where is that turtle? Before that, my net slashed open? This region must be the home of jinn, fairies, and ogres. No one else could have done such a thing. I'd better get out of this place in case someone decides to put a spell on me!

NARRATOR: The hunter returned to the village and told the other hunters his story.

HUNTER: Listen to me brothers; that forest and those fields are inhabited by jinns or fairies or ogres. Don't go near that place, or trouble will follow you!

NARRATOR: After that, no one went to hunt there. And so the four unlikely friends, the mouse ...

ZIRAK: Squeak!

NARRATOR: ... the crow ...

CROW: Caaaa.

NARRATOR: ... the turtle ...

TURTLE: Blub blub. *(Clears throat.)* Ahem.

NARRATOR: ... and the deer ...

DEER: *(Giggles.)*

NARRATOR: ... all four saved themselves from disaster and trouble by cooperating and working together. They lived together in peace and happiness for many long years in that wilderness.

The End

About the Author

Nabeela M. Rehman is a writer and artist with a Ph.D. in Biochemistry. Her short stories have been published in *The Petrichor Review*, *Black Lantern Publications*, *Chautauqua*, *Critical Muslim*, *Bewildering Stories,* and *Literary Mama*.

Printed in Great Britain
by Amazon